A SHORT SEASON

Faith, Family, and a Boy's Love for Baseball

G. DAVE BOHNER & JAKE GRONSKY

D1456855

SUNBURY PRESS

Mechanicsburg, PA USA

Published by Sunbury Press, Inc.
Mechanicsburg, Pennsylvania

www.sunburypress.com

For information about special discounts for bulk purchases, please contact Sunbury Press Orders Dept. at (855) 338-8359 or orders@sunburypress.com.

To request one of our authors for speaking engagements or book signings, please contact Sunbury Press Publicity Dept. at publicity@sunburypress.com.

ISBN: 978-1-62006-022-3 (Trade paperback)
ISBN: 978-1-62006-026-1 (eBook)

Library of Congress Control Number: 2018932078

FIRST SUNBURY PRESS EDITION: March 2018

Product of the United States of America
0 1 1 2 3 5 8 13 21 34 55

Set in Bookman Old Style
Designed by Crystal Devine
Cover by Lawrence Knorr
Edited by Kate Matson

Continue the Enlightenment!

CONTENTS

JOSIAH'S NOTE

Dear friend

I hope you love reading this book as much as I love God and the game of baseball. And most of all, find Jesus!

Remember:
No matter what, fight through it and
Never Give Up!!

JOSIAH VIERA

1

HE'S MY TREASURE

WE DROPPED OUR BAGS on the hotel floor. Josiah and I had finally escaped the blazing sun that made my eyes more wrinkled and weathered from squinting than the sixty years of life I had previously walked. It was March, and the sun in the eighty-five-degree piercing blue sky burned our pale skin raw after exiting a plane from the forty-degree, gray slush pile we called home.

We were in a new world—a world we thought was out of our grasp of reality. The flat, hot, sticky coastline of the sparkling Atlantic Ocean remained a sharp contrast to the bitter cold mountain air of central Pennsylvania. It was a contrast none of us could prepare for.

But then again, all of this was a journey none of us could have prepared for.

"Dave Bohner," I hesitantly said to the woman at the front desk, hoping we were in the right spot.

"Dave . . . Bohner," she repeated, typing my name into the computer. She leaned in and squinted at the screen to double check she wasn't mistaken. "With the St. Louis Cardinals?"

"Yes! That's us!" I shouted as I looked down to my grandson, Josiah, who had the biggest smile on his face, and I couldn't help but join him.

"I have you booked for six nights in our corner suite. You'll be down the hall with the rest of the team."

They must have made a mistake. Six nights?! With the team?! As the words came out of the receptionist's lips, Josiah was giggling with excitement. I graciously thanked her, but I think Josiah's laugh told her more than my words ever could.

We were here; we were finally here.

I glanced around the lobby and my eyes were drawn to the waxed and buffed floors that gave the room a mirror sparkle that highlighted what seemed to be the white-gloves, black tie, reservation-only hotel restaurant. The chapel ceilings of the lobby suspended glass chandeliers and led to each room's poolside string of cabanas just outside of the patio's decadent French doors. We stood in awe of its beauty and elegance and imagined all the kings and queens that had walked on these sparkling floors.

OK . . . maybe a DoubleTree hotel isn't actually as luxurious as it felt, but to us, it was the Ritz-Carlton. The whole experience felt like we were courted by the Queen: flying down for spring training, staying with the team, and three full-access passes to the St. Louis Cardinals just didn't seem possible. But then again, to be standing here after the journey this little boy fought through, our line between possible and impossible has permanently blurred.

The hostess placed our keys alongside two walnut chocolate chip cookies. Before she could hand them to Josiah, we saw two figures walking down the hall. One was taking a sip of water through a protein shaker and the other was burying his head in his phone as the two walked toward the restaurant like robots. But as soon as one saw Josiah, his face lit up: "JV!!"

The name "JV" meant only one thing: They were St. Louis Cardinals baseball players from the 2015 State College Spikes, and as the words leapt out of the player's mouth, the other's head shot to attention and a big smile came to his face.

"Get over here, buddy!"

Josiah took off.

At age twelve, Josiah is twenty pounds and only thirty-six inches tall. He has a bright smile; cute, plump rosy cheeks; and a small voice that can bring the toughest men to their knees. But his fragility comes with a price. His knees bulge over his twig-like legs, exposing skeleton where muscle should be. His ankles wobble and buckle with each step, barely holding his frame. And his transparent pink skin reveals the dark veins running across his face. Just one look shows the harsh reality this little boy faces, but just one laugh shows the joy that remains untouchable.

In the past year, walking had become a challenge. Josiah's strength had started to fade, and his body was deteriorating. His knees bulged more than years past, and the winter had made his hips tighten much faster than we hoped. It's the harsh reality of a terminal illness that no child should have to face, but to Josiah, it's just another day.

Josiah pumped his arms and scooted his legs as fast as he could to see his friends but only gained about six inches with every step. The players covered the rest of the distance and greeted him with a big hug. They said their hellos and initiated the handshakes they had created last season. What was going to be just a mundane dinner routine for the two players had become a cheerful reunion of laughter and hugs.

I looked over to the receptionist, and she tilted her head and frowned. She put her hands over her chest and said, "That is the cutest little boy I have ever seen."

* * *

Our excitement was no longer concealable as we headed toward our room. Josiah giggled all the way through the lobby after seeing his old friends, and his old friends laughed the entire way to their dinner. I pushed our luggage cart over the polished lobby floor and saw a memory of central Pennsylvania: a waterfall. It wasn't much, just a modern accent piece, but I couldn't take my eyes off it.

The thin layer of water running down the face of marble made me smile every time we walked past the lobby during those six days. It drew me back home, reminding me of the beautiful falls hidden within the mountains that defined our family's lives. Not just the Appalachian Mountains, but also the mountains that stood between our family. My fight through a childhood spent in abuse, my daughter's struggle for her family, and Josiah's fight for survival seemed like boulders put in our way that we could never overcome.

Whether we wanted to or not, we were forced to climb them, and with each attempt, and each failure, we grew stronger. We prayed through the difficult days and rejoiced for the good ones; but in the moments of our greatest pain, we found love. Our journey has shown us that salvation is not perfection. Salvation is knowing that tests and trials only strengthen our faith, and through our greatest challenge, we found our greatest hope.

Now when I see the beautiful waterfalls our Appalachian Mountains hold, I no longer see just falling water. I see grace. I see forgiveness. I see a family. And to find the love that we now share as a family, to me, the journey over each mountain was worth every step.

I smiled as we passed the waterfall, but Josiah's excitement quickly turned into a dragging labor of pain. He had almost reached the elevator when his knees began to give.

"Wanna ride on my shoulders?" I said, seeing his legs weakening.

"No."

Usually it would be about halfway down a hallway before his legs fully gave out, but the excitement carried him almost to the first turn. He stopped and tried to take another step, but his knees kept wobbling. He tried to push through, but the more he attempted to move, the more his knees kept buckling. He lowered his head, knowing he couldn't walk any farther. As his frustration led to the realities of a diagnosis a child should never face, Josiah fought back tears.

"It's OK, Bubby. Why don't you just hop on my shoulders until we get to the room, OK?" I delicately said, trying to comfort him using the nickname his older sister, Daisha, coined.

He looked up at me and took a small breath, "OK."

"OK" was the only way he would ask for help. He wanted to be a twelve-year-old boy, but no matter how hard he fought, he was trapped in a body well beyond his nineties. "OK" was his way of screaming in pain. "OK" was his call for help. "OK" was his disappointment at a small defeat.

I lifted Josiah onto my shoulders, and we walked over the sparkling mirror tiles to our room. My key swiped open the door to a room fit for a king, with a fridge, couch, TV, and every other amenity we could wish for. I opened the blinds and shielded my eyes as the harsh Florida sun came rushing in. After my eyes had adjusted, I looked around the complex and smiled as I found the palm trees and cabanas we first spotted through the French doors of the lobby. I turned around, and Josiah was already climbing on the bed, wrestling with the abundance of pillows. We both laughed. It seemed as though paradise was prepped and ready for our arrival, and in some ways, I guess it was.

* * *

The next morning we jumped out of bed and our hearts thumped. Today was the day. Today was the first time we got to experience Major League Spring Training! As usual, we prepared Josiah's bag of medicine and emergency kit: medication for the day, supplies in case of yet another seizure, towels to keep him cool, and water for us both. Josiah was so excited he even slept with his Cardinal uniform on to be ready the moment our morning alarm buzzed. As soon as our feet hit the floor, we grabbed our hats, I tied his sneakers, and we were out the door.

We walked down to the pearly lobby floor and were greeted by the man who paid for all of our expenses to be here, our sponsor, Andy Long. Even today, these trips are only possible with a sponsor because I just can't afford them. The money I made wasn't a lot, but it was enough. Some months are tough, but so is our family. We hit a stretch during my wife's sickness where money just wasn't coming in. I was at home more than I was at work. So I took my retirement from the welding plant early to help take care of my wife. She is a strong-willed woman and insisted she could take care of herself, but my family needed me more than the welding torch did, so I put in my two-weeks' notice. I received a small monthly retirement benefit, but we made it work—it's what we do. We live a simple life, and extravagant vacations just aren't possible.

The Cardinals made sure there were rooms secured for us, but Andy took care of the rest. From transportation to meals, Andy has truly been a blessing to our family, but also a great friend.

We were first introduced to Andy through the Children's Miracle Network, or CMN, the fundraising organization for their network of children's hospitals throughout the country. Andy owns a Subaru dealership in Northumberland, Pennsylvania, and is always looking for ways to help his community. From fundraisers at his dealership, donations to charity, or community service, Andy truly has a heart for helping people.

In early 2014, I got a call from CMN about a fundraising event they wanted Josiah to attend. Their goal is to raise enough money each year to provide advanced surgical equipment, educational materials, special pediatric care necessities, and toys for the children in the hospitals they support. They are a great organization, and without them, I don't know where our family would be right now. We try to help them as much as we can, but we're always a bit weary. We try to do our best to help the organizations that help us, but with all public relations events, we make sure Josiah won't be exploited. He's not a prop and will not be used for donations. I told the CMN rep, Bonnie Tharp, we would think about it and get back to her, but before I could hang up the phone, she quickly replied, "No, you want to be there."

I once again told her I would talk to Josiah and get back to her, but she cut me off, "Trust me, Dave. You really, really want to be there."

Of course she was hinting at something, but I didn't know what. My curiosity got the best of me. I agreed.

We drove to the dealership in our family car, an old short-cab Ford pick-up with the bench seat stretching door to door, and were met by local news reporters, the CMN directors, and the owner of the dealership, Andy Long. We went through the standard media gauntlet—explaining the disease, the challenges Josiah faces, and how the CMN helps. It was an excellent promotion for CMN, and Andy is a big donor to the charity, so it was a great way to give him some well-deserved publicity. Josiah got to ride in their most expensive cars from the showroom and met some great people. It was a nice little gathering. The camera crews left, and as we were inside talking with Andy, he looked out onto the car lot and saw my little truck.

"Is that your work truck?"

"It's all I got. Seats two, but we cram three with the middle console," I said with a small laugh.

"You can't bring your family around in this!" he yelled. "Well I told the CMN I wanted to give your family a gift, but I have a new idea." I curiously leaned over my arm on the table, and he continued: "Pretty soon the kids will be too big to cram into that truck.

I have a client, owns an Outback—one owner, in great condition, and he's trading it in. And I'm giving it to you."

My jaw must have hit the table.

"You're . . . what?"

"Now, it's going to be used, but it's a great family car, and you guys can grow into it."

"Andy. I don't know what to say. Thank you. From the bottom of my heart, thank you so much."

"It's my pleasure. The only problem is, he's not going to trade in until later this year, so I'm gonna give you one of our new loaners. But whenever it gets close to fifteen thousand miles, bring it back and I'll give you another one."

It was the most gracious gift anyone had ever given us. We joked that since I had to take my retirement that year, this was my golden watch. And Andy couldn't have been any more humble: no cameras, no media. I was scrambling to find my phone to call the CMN and get the news reporters back because this was a man who deserved recognition. This was the most sincere act of kindness, and Andy deserved the credit. People needed to see this genuine kindness from a car salesman, of all people—a car salesman! But Andy asked me not to say anything. The CMN knew he was going to give us a gift, but they were not sure what. He told me if it was on the news, people would be lining up for a free car, and with a small laugh and smile he said, "And I'm awful at saying no."

So it became our secret.

Once he gave us the trade-in, he covered all the maintenance, all the oil changes, and anything the car needed. We drove it for two straight years, well over 130 thousand miles. As the transmission faded, Andy told us to bring it in for a check. He looked at the car and said, "Pick any one on the lot."

With a snap of the finger, he gave us yet another car.

"What color does Josiah want?" he said.

"I'll give you three guesses!"

Andy knew right away, and we started walking through the lot of Cardinal-red vehicles.

"How about this Forester?" he said, tapping his hands on the hood. "Brand new, seventeen miles, and is a nice little SUV."

I opened the front door, and like a kid looking at the Christmas gifts under the tree, I couldn't stop smiling as I ran my fingers along the new interior with black trim. I wrapped my hands around the steering wheel and began exploring every gadget on the console. I looked back and saw a seat for everyone in our family—Josiah's car seat on the right, Daisha on the left. This was a life of luxury that I could hardly accept.

"This is perfect." But we both knew this was a car I could never afford and a gesture I could never repay. Andy then said, "Don't worry, we can work this all out for you. Don't worry, it's taken care of."

"Andy, God bless you."

* * *

Andy flew down to Florida with us to experience this special week. We loaded up his rental car and headed toward the spring training home of the St. Louis Cardinals. We were only ever used to minor league baseball. There's a certain feeling driving to our usual home at Medlar Field for the State College Spikes games—anticipation, excitement, a smoldering anxiousness to see the team—but driving to the major league complex of the St. Louis Cardinals felt a little different. We had traded in the scenic mountaintops and evergreens for blue skies and palm trees, and through the orchestra of emotions swirling around the car, the pre-game butterflies in our stomachs strummed the loudest.

We saw the first sign for "The Florida Home to the St. Louis Cardinals," and our hearts jumped. We turned off the highway and down the promenade and drove toward the farm of stadium lights peeking out over the building. Restaurants lined the streets with Cardinal jerseys draped in every window. Cardinal Nation was alive and well in Florida, and we were headed straight for it.

We pulled up to the stadium entrance, and between the arches of what looked to be a baseball coliseum, we saw "Major League Personnel Only," with the Roger Dean Stadium logo underneath. Like the poolside string of cabanas, palm trees lined the brick walkway and workers hustled in and out of the gates in preparation for the one o'clock p.m. first pitch versus the in-stadium-rival, the Miami Marlins. We were starstruck; we were in heaven.

Seeing Josiah's face light up as we pulled into the "Major League Personnel Only" parking was a moment I'll always remember. Maybe it was from everything our family went through—or maybe it was everything Josiah went through—but we learned the hard way that all we have are little moments. Our jobs, our successes, our failures do not define our lives but are only connecting pieces of who we are.

It's not what we do but who we are that matters.

Glory fades, and sorrow ends, and all we are left with are the moments between.

Josiah has been forced to accept so many unforgiving realities—this was his triumph. This was where Josiah belonged: on a field, in a uniform, surrounded by some of the most gifted people in the world. This was his moment in the sun, and it was our moment to cherish.

*   *   *

SPRING TRAINING

Josiah, Andy, and Dave walked through the parking lot and entered Roger Dean Stadium. This was not just a place to house the team for a month of spring training—Roger Dean Stadium is "The Motherland." The Spring Training Home of the St. Louis Cardinals and the Miami Marlins, the stadium houses their short season Rookie-ball and Advanced-A affiliates; front-office executives; the international headquarters for Venezuelan, Puerto Rican, and Dominican Republican baseball academies; the performance center for strength and conditioning staffs; and the major league/minor league rehab center for both organizations. Not to mention the kitchens, cafeterias, operations management, and all the departments needed to run such a big complex. Left-field clubhouse is headquarters for the Marlins operations while the right-field side is the Cardinals. It's a dual-headed octopus with tentacles of baseball fields spanning for miles behind it. The complex is big, confusing, and to three new fans, it was as intimidating as it gets.

The culture of spring training breeds competition. The sandstone plaster walls and wavy red roof tiles give spring training the tropical vacation fans assume. The beach chairs, the Hawaiian shirts, and the constant babble by patronizing broadcasters explaining how players are "just getting their work in today" show the vacation perception we are led to believe.

For the big contract players, this could hold some truth. The three-time All-Stars and the Gold Glove winners do have the luxury of using a month to get back into playing shape, but for the other ninety-nine percent, or two hundred-plus players, spring training is a platform to earn a job. Your team-mates are your opponents, and to keep the jersey on your back, you must outplay them. Everyone knows their jobs are at stake, and for a game built on a team's effort, players become quite individualistic.

For each guy that earns a job, another is cut. Every year over fifty players are given an unconditional release in the final two weeks of spring training, ending their career with that team. So when this trial of competition and uncertainty is described as a "tropical vacation," players cringe.

Uncertainty can also bring excitement, especially for the fringe big-leaguers. A good spring can lead to a promotion over a player that underper-formed, bumping you closer to the dangling golden carrot of the MLB twenty-five-man rosters. It's a test, and spring training is the gauge to measure off-season training, initiate competitiveness, and have player versus player comparisons. Rosters are made, players are cut, and the season begins. Spring training is swift and potent and is the motivating push during a player's offseason.

But high-strung competition forges an attitude. Players are focused and ready to compete against a dozen other players just as skilled and just as talented as they are for a season. The ongoing joke in the minor leagues is that there is more competition within your dugout than the one across the diamond. This motivation can drive players to the big leagues, but it can also drive players crazy. People laugh when psychologists and mental health pro-fessionals leave their business cards in each locker room for services "free of charge," but it's real, and a brutal wake-up call to the stress and pressure a player deals with throughout the season.

Upon entering the clubhouse at 6:30 a.m., the players are greeted by two front-office members standing at the front door. As players leave the bus, ca-sual conversation fades as players notice the personnel in front of the gates. Best-case scenario, you hear nothing. No greeting, no hello, no name. Means you are safe. Worst-case scenario, they say your name. This means you are about to be cut (well, actually, you have been released the night before, and they have already voided your contract, ended your insurance plan, cleared you off the payroll, and your flight home has already been confirmed and boards within the hour). Pack your locker; you leave for the airport in fifteen minutes. Players refer to them as the "Reaper Crew," and if you pass "good morning," it's time to eat breakfast and start your day.

It becomes a routine: wake up at 6:00 a.m., dodge the Reaper Crew, workout until noon, eat lunch, play a game at 1:00 p.m., eat dinner, then go back to the hotel. It's monotonous, it's continuous, and it's the same drills every morning followed by the same anxiety at night. Guessing what moves are happening—who's going where coupled with what so-and-so is doing while trying to find the pulse of the organization's interstellar ideas—makes it tempting to put that mental health professional's business card to good use.

When the team announced a new honorary bench coach named Josiah would be joining the spring training rosters, no one batted an eye. It was business as usual. Rosters still needed to be made, and the Reaper Crew would still be outside the front gate. The line in the sand had been drawn, and no one could break the players' focus; no one could ease their tension.

But when the players met Josiah, the culture began to shift. Players felt a release and freedom they were never searching for. It was more than an inspiration; it was the start of a relationship. The fact that a little boy and his grandfather could stroll into camp and change the perspective of a group of the most elite athletes on the planet no longer made Josiah a charity case; he had become a valuable asset to the St. Louis Cardinals. But frankly, no one knew the magnitude of Josiah's impact until they met him.

* * *

We walked to the clubhouse entrance and were greeted by the Cardinals Player Development and Baseball Operations Coordinator, Tony Ferreira. He got us acquainted with the huge complex and told Josiah the team was waiting for him. We were just in time for Josiah's favorite part of the day: batting practice. Glove in hand, he walked right through the major league doors of the complex and made a beeline for the locker room, leaving Andy and me behind. We were busy making small talk with Tony just waiting for a security guard to come over and inevitably tell us we could not enter. But as we approached another uninviting sign that read in all caps, "MAJOR LEAGUE PERSONNEL ONLY," we walked right through.

I have to admit, I was a bit sheepish walking into a Major League Baseball clubhouse, but my excitement overruled my anxiety, so Andy and I followed Tony inside.

With one look we saw the significance this room held. Wooden lockers of players we spent hours watching on ESPN each night lined the perimeter of a room full of couches, TVs, video games, and a ping-pong table. Imagine that: two fans from Hegins, Pennsylvania, getting to walk past their favorite players from *Sunday Night Baseball* playing ping-pong in sliding shorts and flip-flops. It was very surreal because now we were introduced to our heroes, no longer as players we imitate, but as human beings. As nurturing as it was, we still couldn't help but feel a little bit out of place.

We finally found Josiah talking with his buddies and hanging out with his good friend, Mitch Harris. Now, Mitch wasn't an ordinary Cardinal. He was a standout pitcher for the Naval Academy in 2008 and was drafted by the St. Louis Cardinals in the thirteenth round. He signed, but was unable to play until fulfilling his military commitment. So, after completing four years in the Navy, Mitch Harris was now a twenty-seven-year-old member of the Class A Short Season affiliate, the State College Spikes, and almost a full year older than his manager and now current big-league first base coach, Oliver Marmol. Mitch saw what was extraordinary in Josiah. He didn't see a disease or a charity; like his career with the Cardinals, he saw a second chance.

Andy and I walked over to the kitchen where Mitch and Josiah lounged, grabbing a pregame snack. I still wasn't sure if we were allowed to be in the kitchen, let alone eat the food, but we decided to walk over anyway and just wait until we were kicked out. My heart started pounding when I heard a voice call for me from the clubhouse. This was it; I knew we were going to be asked to leave, so I started looking for the exit.

"Dave," he said, reaching for my hand. "Hey, Dave, how are you?" It was former St. Louis Cardinal and All-Star left fielder, Matt Holliday.

I shook his hand and we reconnected like old friends. We met Matt on our first trip to St. Louis in 2014, and he quickly became one of Josiah's favorites. He's a real gentleman on and off the field, and after shaking hands with him, we couldn't have felt more welcomed.

Once we finished our snack, we headed toward the clubhouse and players started hooting: "Joey V!" "Jooo!" "JV!" Everyone flocked to greet him. It was a warm welcome that brought the biggest smile to his face. We talked with most of the guys, and I was overwhelmed by the reception they gave us. We spend so much time looking up to the players in this very clubhouse on television that we can sometimes forget they are human beings. The connection they have with Josiah stretches far beyond the ball field, and it's a privilege to have them in our lives.

I wasn't the only one to take notice. A reporter from NBC with a temporary clubhouse pass walked up to me and asked, "What's going on?"

He came a little late to the party and missed the welcoming, so I pointed to Josiah and responded, "That's my grandson, Josiah."

"That's him?! I've heard people talk about him, but I never had to chance to meet him," he told me. "Would it be OK if I did a story about Josiah for our St. Louis NBC affiliate?"

And just like that, Josiah and I had cameras following us the next day. Most of the guys headed back to the kitchen for a pregame snack, so we followed. Mitch led us to a table with All-Stars Matt Carpenter, Adam Wainwright, Matt Holliday, and fellow central PA boy, Matt Adams. Matt Carpenter was finishing his morning meal when he gestured toward their personal chef: "Dave, get something to eat." He's the first one in the cages every morning and breaks a sweat before the sun rises, but above his work ethic and All-Star-caliber game, he's a true man of God.

"Well, I don't think—"

"Dave. Go get something to eat and come back," he said in a friendly demand.

So I went to the buffet and ate like a king. Fresh eggs, sausage, bacon, biscuits, and any breakfast food you could imagine filled my plate. I sat back down with the guys, who were already laughing with Josiah, and realized how blessed we truly are.

By the time we got back from breakfast, Mitch was nudging us with a childish grin to head back to the clubhouse. We were in no rush to get back out into the Florida sun, but his giddy laugh of determination for us to walk directly to the clubhouse raised our curiosity. We took one step into the clubhouse and Mitch pointed to a once open and abandoned locker, which now had a white tag with "Josiah" written above it and a small jersey hanging directly under it. Josiah ran to hug Mitch, and my throat tightened as Andy put his arm around my shoulder. It was a subtle touch to an extravagant experience, and it was only the beginning.

*   *   *

We traveled with the team to Field 1 for batting practice, and after a short round of hitting, Josiah was swarmed with Cardinal fans asking for his picture and autograph. Most had heard his story, and now they got to meet him for the first time. It was very humbling—and quite honestly, thrilling—to see my little man be adorned by fans.

After his batting practice, I took out a few of Josiah's baseball cards when we got to the clubhouse and like a shark that smells blood, we couldn't hand them out fast enough. Ten-year veterans, MLB All-Stars, and even players we just met swarmed the table just to get Josiah's baseball card. Our idols became our friends, and for a time, a little boy became their idol. Like the thousands of children they give autographs to every day, every time a player received a card they rushed over to Josiah to be the next one to have it officially autographed. The roles were reversed, and the players were now the fans.

In the midst of passing out dozens of cards, I saw Jaime Garcia in the corner of my eye climbing on his locker. I left the card business to my little man and rushed over to see what he was doing. I got to his locker, and there it was. Josiah's autographed baseball card hanging on his top shelf right next to his baseball glove.

With a smile, he looked at me, pointing to the newest addition to his locker.

"Now every time I pitch, I'm gonna get a little more inspiration from my little man."

I couldn't help but gaze at the card, realizing that it no longer was just a thin cardboard photo of Josiah, but a message to push forward. I thanked Jaime for being such a good role model and looked around the clubhouse. Players began putting Josiah's card in their lockers, and now we saw that like every other trip Josiah had been on, this was no longer a charity event. The message that was now resonating through the hearts of the St. Louis Cardinals was not a feeling of happiness, but an invitation to live beyond a situation and find the joy in their lives they've been missing. Everyone here had seen the pain Josiah goes through. They saw him struggling to walk, they saw his scars, they saw his fragile body, and through all his hurt, they saw his strength. They saw inspiration. This was no charity case; this was a gift.

* * *

As the players headed to the field for their matchup against the Marlins, we decided to give Josiah's mother, my daughter Jen, a call to tell her about our trip. We told her about the flight, hotel, players, food, and spilled all the details to her like two elementary school kids on a field trip.

She couldn't be happier.

I could hear it in her voice that she was genuinely floored by the love and appreciation her son continued to receive and was thankful for the story of triumph he had been able to share. She was in a good place and had finally found the love in her life she had been searching for.

That was the Jen I know.

Her affection and desire to bring the world to her family's doorstep were the missing pieces of my daughter I thought I had previously lost. Jen's a tall, country-strong woman born in central Pennsylvania and is my beautiful girl. Undoubtedly she got her good looks from her mother's side and only inherited a hardheaded stubbornness and hairpin fuse from mine. But the strength and courage you see today is not how it has always been. The more I yelled during her teenage years, the more she wanted to run, and after the miserable eighteen years of life I gave to her, I didn't blame her.

I wish I had been there for her; I wish I understood her, but I only pushed her away. At times I thought I had lost her, and after receiving the death sentence of her only son, I worried she was too far gone. But the pain we faced was the pain we shared, and although things may not have ever been perfect, during our weakest moments we found a way to love each other. Through a little boy's fight toward health, we found a way to forgive.

On that phone call, I had heard the voice of my daughter—a mother, a loving partner, and the person I've always wanted to know. She was in a good place, and so were we.

*   *   *

Seeing "Birds on the Bat" draped across my little boy's chest was a sight that will never blur and a memory that will never fade. It's hard to describe the excitement, the joy, the humility, the love of seeing your own grandson sit in a major league clubhouse, in his own locker, wearing his own jersey.

We had just finished getting him ready for the upcoming exhibition game, and as soon as I tied the last loop on his shoes, he ran off with the team and headed for pregame stretch. I took a seat in his locker and kept a minute to myself. Maybe I was a little hesitant to head back out into the pounding Florida heat, or maybe I needed to stop and see the glory in that moment. Sitting there, I felt some of my own life was wrapped up in that little man God sent us. He has more spunk and tenacity than most people I know, including myself, and was finally where he belonged: among the greats.

I sat in Josiah's locker, absorbing all that a major league locker room had to offer, and looked at Josiah's bat bag hanging in the clubhouse of legends. Holliday, Carpenter, Wainwright, and all the guys we spent hours each night watching on TV were within an arm's length away, and I couldn't help but think that God made Josiah with the same purpose and mission as the rest of the big-leaguers in this room.

While I sat and took in everything Josiah had fought through to make it to this point, a clubhouse worker walked in. He was starting his daily routine of tidying the room and restocking each locker with towels before the players returned, and he saw me sitting alone. He had a casual smile resting on his face below a pair of thick meaty-framed glasses, and as he neared Josiah's locker, his smile grew. He looked in my direction, and we shared a mutual welcome. Continuing down the row of lockers with a big shopping cart full of towels he nodded his head looking around the clubhouse and joked, "Man, you can make a lot of money selling the treasures in here."

We both giggled, and before he could return to his crate of towels, I leaned over the chair with a big smile and said, "No, sir. There is nothing here worth more than my family and that little man. He's my treasure."

PART 1

THE END

2

COMA PART 1: THE BEGINNING

FOUR HOURS. TO ME, an eternity. But to the world, his surgery was just four hours. The world never understood us, nor did it care. In four hours, the world saw us stare at the face of the clock and heard the click of the minute hand shutter throughout the room.

But the world didn't stop.

The world never heard our silence resonating louder than any click that minute hand could deliver. The world couldn't remember the tears this family shed the day Josiah was diagnosed, and the world could never understand the pain this little boy has been through.

The world will forget us one day, but everything the world would forget, we remember.

The silence was finally broken as the waiting room door sprang open. My heart thumped. Breath shortened.

Dr. Scorpio appeared and told us he had found the reason for Josiah's eating problem. He was a sure-handed surgeon freshly hired from CHOP, a prestigious pediatric hospital in the country, and was assigned to Josiah's case previously in 2005 to reposition the feeding tube as well as the central lines that were previously botched. We met him briefly as he was caught up to speed with Josiah's case and were greeted by his stern, no-nonsense personality. He was straightforward, honest, and unemotional in the pursuit of discovering why this little boy couldn't be fed. It was black and white to him—he was determined to find a solution to Josiah's eating problem, alongside his gastroenterologist, Dr. Cochran, and we couldn't have been more confident with the both of them working side by side.

They told us the news.
It was worse than we expected.

*   *   *

The day we heard the diagnosis our lives changed; or rather, we changed. The people we thought we were had left and we had become someone else—something different. The days were heavy and the nights were long as we wrestled with the diagnosis; or, it wrestled with us.

We studied everything. The newest research, the potential treatments, even alternative therapies and a better timeline, but we only found the news we were trying to spare ourselves from: rapid aging, a steady decline—death.

It was hard to comprehend anything after that. Once we understood, our lives were numb and dulled to the point where we only saw the outside world through a fog. I don't know if you can say we were sad, or angry, or upset, but we became different people. Food was just a necessity, work was just a place, and visiting our little boy in the hospital became our identity. We no longer looked in the mirror and saw who we once were but rather who we were forced to become.

The smallest amounts of happiness became worn, used pieces of time that were spent hollow—simply a placeholder as we waited for another devastating diagnosis. We even used to look forward to what the Child Life Services had in store. Every day they'd have magic shows, sing-a-longs, little games the patients could play to keep the floor as happy and playful as they could. We looked forward to those times with Josiah but more for Daisha, Josiah's fearless and loving older sister. She was only a child, and her sweetness was still pure and one of the only treasures of our lives that wasn't swallowed whole by this hospital and this new life. Woody, as he was called, would come in with his guitar and sing songs for Josiah and Daisha. Josiah, with binky in mouth and legs through the bed rails, would rock back and forth while Woody strummed his guitar, and Daisha would dance alongside Josiah's bed. Even at age one, Josiah's big smile was apparent to all the nurses and doctors, and hearing them speak of its radiance made our days that much better.

But now it was an emptiness we felt.

Josiah still smiled, but we had to force a grin to whatever song was playing. He didn't know his life was any different or that he was given a death sentence, but now everything about the hospital had changed, and we had absorbed the pain he couldn't.

Every smile he gave, every giggle we heard just twisted a knife deeper into our hearts as we knew Josiah was slowly but steadily being ripped away from our arms. Joy left us, and the diagnosis knocked us to our knees; the moment Dr. Scorpio stepped into the waiting room, our lives changed forever. But change has no virtue. It's the only inevitability of life, and it's never easy to bear. For us, as the initial sting of the diagnosis faded away, the unknown set in, and we began a journey that we never agreed to trek. Pain usually logged most of the miles, but somehow—in some way—every step in pain brought us one step closer toward healing.

For the entire year, we did our best to bring our home to him. We dressed him in normal clothes from the house—he had his favorite blanket and his favorite musical toys we used to help him go to sleep. We tried to give him every sense of the word "home" and find ways to enjoy our life together. But the diagnosis was only the beginning, and small proceedures placing central tubes directly into Josiah's stomach to help him gain weight became his only reality.

Then we were told he was going home. It wasn't a celebration. The future was still uncertain for our little boy, but all we wanted to do was scoop him in our arms and carry him to his home. But as Daisha and I returned to the hospital from our home to finally take him in our arms, Jen noticed a dark substance around his feeding tube on his pajamas. She opened the crib to investigate. The brown substance was bowel, and her heart sank once again. Dr Scorpio immediately came in to see Josiah. He looked at Josiah, then looked to his team.

"Josiah needs emergency surgery," he said, and our world changed.

So, for four hours we sat in the waiting room, and for four hours, we sat without the world.

* * *

We ran over to Dr. Scorpio, and like usual, he gave us the cold, honest truth. He called it a malrotation. It was a birth defect detaching his intestines from his abdomen allowing them to twist shut when he ate. It was completely unrelated to the diagnosis and should have been caught a long time ago.

"I've fixed the problem, and I'm confident he will have no more trouble eating without a feeding tube," Dr. Scorpio told us confidently.

"That's good news!" I said with a deep exhale of relief. But Dr. Scorpio wasn't smiling. "Right?"

He took a breath and looked me, and then Jen.

"Josiah has developed the worst kind of abdominal infection you can have. He has just been so weak and so damaged in the past year that we might not ever find out if the surgery was a success."

Stool bubbling out of his tube had caused an infection that had rapidly spread, and Josiah's malnourished body just couldn't defend itself. For the past year, Josiah had fought an endless cycle of sickness that was threating his life. Like he set out to do, Dr. Scorpio fixed the problem and flushed the stool, but Josiah's skin was too brittle and too thin to close and remained exposed. With each possible option, Geisinger's resident, Dr. Walsh, and the medical team suggested—a skin graft, wraps, transplants, etc.—every idea was shot down. A body too weak to sustain itself is a body too weak for a transplant, so the decision was made to leave the surgical site open, now exposing his entire body to the deadly infection.

"I'm sorry," Dr. Scorpio continued explaining. "If only I could've gotten to him sooner . . . I'm afraid we may not ever find out if the surgery was successful. I'm sorry." He paused, making his already stern voice feel like a gavel hammering on my ears.

"Josiah is in the PICU and was put into a coma. He won't last more than a few days."

3

HIS MONSTER

TRYING TO FIND THE Pediatric Intensive Care Unit to see your grandson is something we never believed would happen to us. It was a fictional story; a fable we were never actually meant to live. But we walked through the hospital, and reality set in. This was our life, and this was Josiah's future.

We rode the elevator down to the first floor and passed the final reminder of what our children's hospital room 282 home used to look like—a fuzzy bear painting on the wall that we couldn't help but notice. But like the life we once had, that too was now gone. No more colorfully painted walls, no more yellow playhouses on treasure map carpet; we walked into the standard-issue hospital room. We walked in to his deathbed.

We were buzzed in like visitors at a state penitentiary, and now a dull white- and beige-colored hallway became the fuzzy painted bear paintings we were already missing. We checked in at the desk, but no words were said; rather, no words could be said.

The nurse took us down a dull hallway in a thick silence. I looked around the hall at machines and computers connected to children that seemed to be suspended in a state of limbo traveling between this world and the next. Some were healthy and recovering from whatever it was that brought them here, but some families gripped onto the only life their child had left, and I couldn't stand the sight of it.

The buzz of Geisinger's Janet Weis Children's Hospital, which we called Children's Two, was just a distant memory of the past year and had been traded for the quiet whisper of the PICU. Words were hard. Nurses spoke to each family as gently as families spoke to their children. The solitude was uneasy, creating a divide between thoughts and words, turning my mind into a battlefield between life and death. I wanted someone to talk, or to say something to break the drowning silence, but people just grazed by each other with an unspoken understanding. They didn't need to welcome anyone. They didn't need to ask why they were here. Everyone just understood. This was our new home, our new neighborhood, and the new world Josiah entered.

We walked only a few steps from the circulation desk, but it felt like an eternity. With every stride, I stared at the ground, trying to avoid looking at the families in each passing room, and I couldn't take my eyes off the floor. The scratched walkway of the cold, white floor seemed to tell the story of everyone in that unit. I saw each mark, every indentation highlighted from the fluorescent lights above, and I felt the emptiness of everyone walking over it.

To me, each scuff held a story. I imagined each one to be some frantic emergency only later to be wiped clean and forgotten, then coupled by hundreds more. I imagined the medical staff and the patient—their panic and crisis. I saw the families and their fear for what was about to happen. With each step the floor revealed the life it contained, and I couldn't help but think the scars on the floor would most certainly match the scars on these families' hearts. I heard all the prayers. I saw the families on bended knee. And for some, I knew the only answer would be the silence of a passing child.

I saw the scuffs and I saw the scars, and I started to wonder, would that be our fate? Would this be the last place we ever see our little boy? Would Josiah become another scratch, another life to merely fade away and be forgotten by the world?

The nurse came to a stop, and we read the thin, black, neatly printed "Viera" on the temporary dry-erase board that was ready to be wiped clean at any moment.

"He's here," she whispered.

The nurse must have made a mistake. *Josiah was sick, but not this sick, right?* He had only ever been here after surgery until they always scheduled him back to room 282 the day after. *He can't be here; he fought too hard to end up like this.*

Jen got to the room before I did, and when her eyes met mine, words escaped us. I drew a breath into my lungs and turned to look at Josiah. Jen held her little boy's hand while a stream of wires and tubes ran throughout his seemingly lifeless body. He looked so battered I thought the tick of the minute hand was all that would measure how much time he had left. He was weak, the weakest I've ever seen him, and the very sight of my daughter holding onto all Josiah had left made me crumble. It all finally became real.

This was not a mistake.

This was Josiah, and this was all we had left.

The nurse took us through a brief orientation: Don't touch this, don't worry about that; this is what that's for, that's what this is for; and call this person for that. All very confusing and quite overwhelming for a family member seeing their child like this for the first time, but it was standard procedure. She explained the sirens and the noises on the floor—something the nurses and staff had become numb to over the years—and explained what happens during an emergency and where to go to wait.

We were thrown into controlled chaos, and even with the countless number of emergency calls I had answered over the years, it was no help. When your family is on the wrong side of a hospital bed, everything is the unknown.

Then a machine wheezed to life. Josiah had been hooked to so many machines the past year, wires and tubes had become an extension of his own body. But this one was different; this one scared us. The machine pushed air into his lungs then promptly sucked it back out—all day, all night—*in and out, in and out.* It gave him his breath, but in return it collected his life. This monster seemed to be the only thing keeping him lingering in this world, and with every minimal breath it gave, like a vacuum, it sucked it back out, leaving him as empty as the push before. It was his life support; and it was the only thing alive in the room.

In and out, in and out.

* * *

For the rest of the day, the only sounds that broke the thick silence were the persistent puffs of the ventilator or the soft banter of nurses finishing their rounds. This little boy the size of my extended hand had barely taken a breath outside of hospital walls, and now he lay in the PICU—helpless, frail—and all we could do was watch him wither away.

Is this the end? It was as if each day in the hospital became a test of faith, and each minute became miles swimming across the Atlantic. The swim had worn us down, tired us to the point where treading water became thrusting all of our power into one final push to breach the surface to only draw a quick breath before sinking back under.

We bobbed for air: *He will fight this. I feel it in my bones that this little boy will survive.*

I sunk back under: *God, please. If you want him, take him, but not now. Not yet.*

Our test in faith was no longer propelling forward; I was splashing.

Our faith was tested to the limit, but as I stumbled over my own understanding, I thought back to Job 13:15: "Though He slay me, yet will I trust in Him." I repeated those words over and over again in my head as I meditated on the story of a man who had everything taken from him, yet his faith remained. Job's faith was not of this earth, it was not in his own mind—it was within something greater. Faith is not something tangible we can receive and wait for it to work its magic on our lives. Faith is a leap. It's nothing we can hold or see, but everything we can feel—and we must be bold enough to seek it.

To some extent we all fear death, but the ability to see past it and understand the eternal life we can have in Jesus Christ can comfort us. It's seeing a distant light in a room of darkness and running straight for it. By God's eye, life is but a vapor. It is here for a moment and then vanishes.* We are a snapshot in an eternity of time.

So we must push.

We must leap.

We must see past death.

And we must hope.

---

* James 4:14: *Why, you do not even know what will happen tomorrow. What is your life? You are a mist that appears for a little while and then vanishes.*

Our faith is not something our world can give us. Our faith is in the One who gives us eternal life.

Josiah belonged to God, and on that painful day in the PICU, I realized that this special little man was only given to us on loan. It was this hope that kept us all alive in that PICU hospital room, and it was this hope that I knew could save a little boy's life—because it had saved my own.

4

MOM, CHURCH IS DEAD

I RODE IN THE back of a funeral car with my newly widowed stepmom—his second wife, her second marriage—in all black, like we were supposed to be mourning something. We sat in silence, as the constant rev of the engine crawling up and down the rolling hills of Pennsylvania was the only noise to break the solitude. We had never spoken much before, so why should this car ride be any different? She sat unfazed by the circumstance that brought us together and didn't drop a tear at her own husband's funeral. But I guess the feelings were shared because neither did I.

Later in his life, I visited him two or three times a week. Back then, I only lived a block away, but it might as well have been a thousand miles. We didn't have a father-son relationship. We would sit in his kitchen for a short while and talk shop over toast and a cup of coffee. I worked for a company that my dad managed for twenty-six years, so my conversations with him were more like talking with a co-worker. When an issue would arise within the family, he tuned it out. That was not a point for discussion.

He had a new life and didn't want to admit what had happened in the old. After a while, it was like talking to a stranger. There were times when I thought—well, hoped—I could have a dad or just a father that would say "I love you," but I knew better. Those three words never came out of his mouth, and by the time my cup was cold, I was out the door.

I saw him a few weeks before he died and he looked terrible. He never took care of himself, but this time was different. His eyes were weak, as if fully opening his eyelids took strength he no longer had, and as I looked down, his toes were blue. I knew right away: diabetic neuropathy had set in. It was only a matter of time.

But I didn't say anything. I didn't care.

The awkward car ride with his widow stopped, and we pulled up to a small gravesite through a row of thinning trees. I think we both shared a sigh of relief stepping out of that stuffy car ride. We were now one step closer to getting this ceremony over and getting on with our lives.

My uncle Bob was already there, waiting for the preacher and standing motionless off at a distance with my two sisters and my brother standing in his full army dress uniform. I leaned against a tree nailed with a wooden picket sign that read "Fresh Flowers Only" and scoffed under my breath. Whoever brought this man a flower in his death never saw this man during his life, and now this all became real. The sickening feeling that lived in my stomach my entire childhood came back. I couldn't check my watch quick enough to get this thing over.

* * *

It started in a small row home apartment and shortly moved a few doors away into the Delany Mansion located on the east side of Lykens, PA. It was the American dream: A big beautiful house and a loving stay-at-home wife to a husband on the board of directors of a worldwide company with a family growing up slow in a small rural town in Pennsylvania. It was the story people grew up on: A man without a high school education pulls himself from poverty and gives his family the life of luxury.

I envy people with a dad because I never had one. I had a man who was legally my parent, but I never considered him my father. By the time he found out another child was on the way, my brother was already fighting a war in Korea and my oldest sister was out of the house, though my closest sister still lived at home. Needless to say, I was well beyond an afterthought; I was the unwanted baby.

Later in life, I recalled being told a somewhat unbelievable story. He tried to sell me to the highest bidder. There was a local doctor who was rumored to deliver babies like a surrogate and sell them to infertile couples for profit, and like the businessman he was, my father tried to strike a deal. I wanted to tell him that he ruined my life, that he should have been a good father and sold me away from him. I could have grown up somewhere away from him, and maybe I could have had a decent home.

I should have said it.

I never had the guts.

I looked around, and the funeral was over. Still leaning next to the "Fresh Flowers Only" sign, I didn't even realize the ceremony had happened. No one cried, no one mourned, no one even said any final words. It was just a passing vapor, and like the lives he gave to us, we all wanted it to end.

My father didn't die that day—just a man I once knew and nothing more.

The night he passed, my stepmom had handed me a green safety deposit box and said I could have it. I opened it up. There were a few papers from work hiding beneath his beloved trigonometry equation—his spiral heat exchanger formula that gave him the promotion of his dreams—and a pocket watch. I thought the watch was his retirement gift, but it wasn't until a few years later when I opened the box again and realized it was an Elgin. They stopped production on those watches long before my father retired, and I realized after some research that it was a conductor's watch purchased in 1939, with nineteen jewels beautifully wrapped inside the gold-plated facing. My dad once told me he was a railroad engineer with the Philadelphia & Reading Railroad prior to WWII. Whether it was true or not, I didn't care. It was nice, and I wanted to sell it, but instead I just put the watch in the box alongside his formula and tucked it away forever. It was finally over. Thank God, it was finally over.

Or so I thought.

Weeks after his funeral, my closest sister started her shift at the local grocery market, and two men, members of the board at the local bank, carried on small talk. As the conversation was beginning to simmer, one man looked at my sister as if to perk up the conversation and said, "By the looks of it, you guys should be taken care of for the rest of your—" His partner quickly nudged him and whispered something in his ear.

"Oh, I'm sorry, ma'am," the man recovered. "I must be mistaken."

And the two men scurried off.

It was an abrupt ending to the conversation, and it just didn't sit right with my sister. She was furious when she told me what had transpired. Later, my sisters were told there were insurance policies and retirement savings, all left to his stepfamily. All except for a trigonometry equation and antique pocket watch.

We never wanted his money—or his pocket watch. We only wanted our childhood, his love, or at least the feeling that we were good enough.

Before he died, however, I told him I wanted his Winchester model 70-bolt action rifle with the unfinished walnut stock. He knew exactly which one, too. It was his best gun; could shoot one hundred yards open sight and was the only gun we'd shoot together. The time we spent on the mountainside was the best memory we shared and was the only part of my childhood I wanted to hold onto. Strangely enough, I actually thought he enjoyed those moments, too. I loved that gun, and it was the one possession of his that meant something to me, so I asked him if I could have it. But like everything else in our lives, he didn't care. To him, we were just there. We were just people in his way. Once he started a new family, he started over and left us behind.

He gave that gun to someone else in his new family soon after that day.

* * *

I don't know how he did it or how he got away with it. He was an alcoholic, but I guess a big job and a beautiful home covered up the brutal abuse he gave us. After dinner, we'd see the garage lights come on and we knew he was home.

Most nights he'd come home drunk and the other nights he'd come home obliterated. On one of those obliterated nights, he was hanging out the car door window, as he popped the door loose and stumbled out. Mom tried to hustle me upstairs, but it was too late. He barged into the house, and I curled up behind Mom's chair, hoping he didn't see me and would just stumble to his room. My mother would always try to rush him up the stairs before he realized we were home. She did her best, but most of the time it was no use.

My mother was a sweet lady, though I never knew it. By the time I was old enough to get to know her, I was shut off from the world. People were just things I didn't understand, and family was just a word I feared.

But Sundays were the best.

Roast beef, hot lettuce, bacon dressing, and sweet potatoes right after church. Mom was an excellent cook, and it was the perfect day. We'd get all dressed up in the morning, go to the local traditional church with our family friends, and listen to the preacher. I sat there and smiled. I genuinely loved church; not because of what the pastor said, but I knew I would go home to a quiet household for a few hours. I knew my sister and I were safe. It was just a façade, but I didn't care. I loved Sundays.

My brothers and sisters all grew up and fled the house as soon as they could. They had to; I truly believed it was the only way they could survive. My father held onto pain and passed it down to us like a generational heirloom making sure each child received the same equal burden, and I undoubtedly pulled it in with two hands.

I don't remember much about my older sister. Like my brother, she was thirteen years older, and the only memories we shared were the ones we tried to forget. But my other sister—the one closest to me in age—she took the worst of it. She rebelled as soon as she could and tried to escape out the front door when the violence started. Sometimes she would reach the door, and others she didn't even get past his right arm, knocking her flat on the floor. But as she got older and faster, she'd make an escape through the alley where he could never find her. I never knew where she went, and I never wanted to ask her. I was just happy she was safe. When he would come home drunk or in a blackened rage, she would sometimes have to fight. It wasn't just for herself; she'd fight for both of us. She was a tough girl and a good sister.

One day after school, my sister wasn't there to protect me. The neighborhood boys and I just got done shooting beer bottles with our BB guns over the train tracks and were back at my house, striking matches. We were pyros; we loved watching the match burn down the stick until the flame touched our fingertips before we'd drop the match in the sand pit. It was our kind of fun, and like shooting beer bottles, we were just kids being kids.

Our sand pit sat between the corner of our house and the overhang of our entryway to the basement. It was where we kept all the old cardboard boxes to throw away, but it was also right underneath the kitchen window.

I struck a match and started burning a long strip of cardboard from our garbage pile and watched the small flame travel across its border. I dropped it into the sand pit and the embers slowly faded into a crusty black char. Without warning, I heard Anthony yell, "Dave, stop it! He's coming, he's coming!" I tried to turn around to see what he was screaming about, but before I could stand up, I felt a hand grip the back of my neck and throw me to the ground. A sudden crack hit me in the ribs, and the whipping of what sounded like a stick cut through the air, striking me in the stomach.

Before he emerged from the back door, he grabbed the end of his fishing rod to give me a beating I would never forget. He wasn't even drunk yet; this was just who he was. I screamed while he whipped me harder and harder and Anthony bore witness. Then on his backswing, he carelessly slapped Anthony in the face, and a red gash opened across his cheek. He ran off to get his father and left me alone at the mercy of another attack.

I felt so bad about playing with matches I couldn't even think about doing it again, but this beating was not about matches. It was about tipping the scales. The small victories my sister fought for didn't sit well, and this was his way of showing it.

I don't remember much after that. I ran inside and saw Anthony's dad coming over to talk with mine. It looked civil, like a debate, or a conversation hashing out small details to a new business deal. But how could any of this be civil? With tears drying on my cheeks I wondered how a man so vicious could be reasoned with as if what he did was just normal. But as I rubbed my eyes, the mild conversation was over, and I realized no one cared. What he had been doing to this family was now our typical life, and even to the rest of the neighborhood, it was accepted. My sister moved in with my aunt across town and married soon afterward.

Unfortunately, I never took the time to thank her and tell her how much I loved her.

* * *

Anger and resentment became my world. Not just toward that man, but my mom, too, for allowing that man to ruin our lives. The abuse wasn't as bad as I got into my early teen years—or maybe it had just started to become my norm—but I stopped caring about church, I stopped talking to my family, and I stopped caring about life.

I didn't care about God, but for some reason, I would still try to talk to Him. I guess I just wanted someone to hear me, someone to save me. And even though every wish remained unanswered, every Sunday I was still forced to sit through a service in a church that didn't care about me and then share a meal with the people I hated most.

Sunday was just another day.

I hated Sundays.

* * *

I couldn't have been older than eight years old when my father showed me my first pornographic magazine. He was addicted to porn my entire life, and it drove my mother crazy. He would always have strange publications lying around, and I was confused by what I was seeing. It bothered me and made me uncomfortable each night after having seen something so graphic. I didn't understand what I was looking at, but I knew he shouldn't have shown them to me and it began to haunt me.

It got to the point where I couldn't speak. Each day I'd walk through the hallways staring at the ground, looking at the herd of feet trampling around, trying to stay out of the way. I thought I was forgotten. Just a mistake that never belonged. In fourth grade I started pulling out my hair. The porn, the abuse, and the isolation built walls between the world in which I was living and the actual world turning without me. Trichotillomania. A type of impulsive control disorder—a medical term I would learn much later in life. I'd sit in my room at night and one by one rip patches of hair from my head, then my eyebrows, and then my eyelids. I was numb, and like a firm poke to check a dead animal for a sign of life, this was my poke. My attempt to feel anything—to discover if I even existed. To take away the pain.

My sister was gone, and it was my turn to face his addiction and anger. He had won. We no longer had my sister as our leader, and I believed I no longer had a chance. At my young age, I felt trapped. Trapped in some kind of nightmare I didn't understand and couldn't escape.

He was a whiskey drinker—the type that would walk into a bar and drink the entire bottle before sitting down. So when he got home, in my mind, it was self-preservation. I became good at hiding as time went by. But some nights when it got bad and I could hear him yelling or arguing with Mom, I found myself curled in my bed, door shut, covered with my blanket, avoiding the life I never asked for. I guess you could call that "situational avoidance," but I was still frightened by what he might do next. I didn't understand all the anger that surrounded me. Little did I know, or even understand, the anger around me was now becoming part of my life.

*   *   *

One Saturday afternoon I was playing with a few toys in my room and he yelled up to me to clean something up, but I refused. I hated being told what to do, even if I did leave my bike outside. I hated confrontation, and I hated that man. So whatever he was telling me to do, I wasn't listening.

He yelled up again for me to come down, and this time, angrily, I slammed the door. But as the door snapped closed I heard his shoes start stomping up the stairs, and I knew I had made a terrible mistake. As he raced toward my room, I could hear him yelling my name through a cloud of nonsense, and I frantically tried to lock my door and hide under the covers. I peeked through my blanket and looked out the window, trying to find an irrational escape, but by the time I realized the jump was too high, he was at the door.

Bang! Bang! Bang!

He pounded the door, yelling at me to open the door at once, and my heart was beating through my chest. The same knot from that night on the basement stairs found my stomach once again, and I froze.

"Open this door, now!" he screamed.

Bang! Bang! Bang!

I pulled the covers tighter around my body, as if the thin cloth would shield me from the nightmare that was about to come true. My panting breaths dampened the air and now my heartbeat was resonating throughout my body.

Then finally—*Bang!*

He smashed the door open and stormed directly toward my bed. He pried the blanket from my grip, and I tried to fight back.

It was useless.

He attacked me until my pain gave him the pleasure he was seeking. I tried to yell for help, but no one heard me; no one cared—at least, so I thought.

In the midst of the beating, I heard my mother frantically yelling, "Stop it! Stop it!" from down the stairs, and to my surprise, he did. My mother's desperate call to end the abuse somehow struck a nerve with this man, and he obliged. Even though my voice—my life—wasn't worth enough to get that man off me, I didn't care. At least it was over.

I grabbed my blanket from the floor and curled up into a ball. Aimlessly staring around my room, I looked at the cross sitting on my dresser and touched it. I didn't know why it was important to me. I didn't care about God or whatever that X was, but it was my only comfort. At night I'd look at it, talk to it, and beg it to make that man stop beating us; but I knew that was just a wish. It was just a plastic glow-in-the-dark cross from a church I hated. But it never left my bedside.

It never moved.

* * *

The abuse ended as I entered my teenage years. It got to the point where that man began to realize I was bigger than him, and he knew if he tried to come near me, this time he would be on the wrong side of the beating. I rebelled as soon as I grew. I put on the "tough guy" act and lived life by my own will, on my own terms, in my own way. He even tried to be Mr. Nice Guy, but I saw through it. We were now on a level playing field. No more hitting; no more abuse. At some point in my later teenage years, he stopped his excessive drinking. But the damage had already been done.

I would lash out at everyone except my friends. The only time I was able to forget about the pain that man put us through was with them. They were my escape, and they stuck with me through thick and thin.

The family I grew up with was just the people our roof contained, and I would scream and yell if things weren't the way I liked. I patrolled the house like the man in my childhood did, and before I could blink; I slowly but steadily was accepting our family's generational heirloom.

But Mom took the worst of it. I'd scream at her almost every day for the tiniest things even though she loved and protected me more than I knew. I guess it was the God thing that bothered me the most. After everything that man put us through, after all the pain and suffering cast onto us, she still went to that fake mainline church and partook in some form of religion. I had stopped going. God had forgotten this family, and I was not about to make Him remember.

*   *   *

I walked into the living room to Mom watching Billy Graham on television, and it infuriated me. I believe my mom knew God, but like me, she was searching for the peace that only Jesus can give. At that time neither of us understood what it meant to have faith in our hearts, and even though she watched Billy Graham devotedly, she didn't understand.

But she never wanted to fight. She was the sweetest lady I never got a chance to know, and today she only wanted to watch Billy Graham, but I had other plans. As she watched the sermon, I decided to sit down next to her and make a mockery of it with every breath. I giggled at every "God bless you" or "Amen" and rolled my eyes at every line of scripture he read as if it were a fairy tale who's spell no longer gripped me. Finally, I snarled at his standing ovation, and Mom gave me the motherly look of disappointment. She stared at the TV and then slowly lowered her head and said, "You should start coming to church with us again."

I wasn't about to have this conversation, so I stood to leave, but she insisted, "David, you really should come."

I turned back. Mom saw the hell we were put through as kids and knew my views on the church. The fact that she had the audacity to tell me what to do sent hot coals running down my spine. I stood directly in front of the television, blocking her sight of Billy Graham signing off to thousands of people hanging on his final words. As the thunderous applause started to blare from the television, I leaned over her chair and gripped the armrests until my knuckles turned white. "She turned away, afraid of the monster I had become. I put my face directly in front of hers and as I looked into her eyes I saw a small line of tears begin to form. I looked at her with the same venom that man used to look at me with, and in the same hate he spoke to us, I said, "Mom, church is dead."

5

COMA: PART 2

WITH EACH MOMENT, JOSIAH'S life was drifting away. Since the day Josiah entered the hospital, we had spent more time within those cement walls than beyond them. He still lay there motionless, as lifeless as the day before, with no medicine left to try and no solutions left to find. Josiah weighed just two pounds, a body suffering from pneumonia, and his life remained dependent on a ventilator.

The doctors tried to flush the fungus out from his intestine one more time, but it was no use. The infection continued to grow and steadily shut down his organs.

Once the feeding tube was directly inserted into his lower intestine, his skin was too tight and too fragile to piece together, and the surgical site remained open. Like trying to sew into tissue paper, his skin couldn't handle stitches, so the doctors could only cover the gaping hole with bandages. Dr. Scorpio continued to check on Josiah's stomach like a football coach would check on his star quarterback. He was quick, efficient, and looked for solutions rather than trying to hold our hand through problems.

"It's just too swollen," he would mutter to us. "I just can't close it."

So, they would rewrap the wound, and without being able to close it, like dirt in a scab, the infection kept spreading. But their hands were tied. That was all they could do to help our little boy. Dr. Walsh would try to concoct a new theory to pitch to Dr. Scorpio in order to attempt a closing procedure, but with each breath, the hardened surgeon would shoot down the resident and move on to the next patient. He was fierce and remained stern, but he would have tried anything to heal Josiah—he just couldn't close it, and he didn't dwell on it. Like the thirty-year veteran surgeon he was, he would just find the next case and press on.

Being told our child's hourly battle for life was slowly fading made us question how much longer he could fight, and our hearts were pulled from our chests wondering how much longer we could let him suffer like that. Every day we came to the hospital, we somehow tried to prepare to say goodbye.

I never questioned God or His sovereignty, but I just didn't know how much more this family could take. I wanted an explanation. I wanted some sort of reason, or at least something.

I held Josiah's hand and sat on a pleather white chair wondering if this was it; if this was the last hospital room and the last place Josiah would ever be, and I bowed my head to pray.

God, if You want him now, take him—I don't know why—but if You want him, he's in Your hands.

I struggled to find the right words but hoped God would show us a sign, a message, or anything to tell us that He heard us. Our family had been knocked down so many times I didn't know if we would ever be able to stand again. But the Lord will never give man that which he cannot handle so I knew we could persevere, but we needed a miracle; and in a moment of weakness, I needed a sign.

So I prayed harder than I ever had. I prayed with faith. I prayed with conviction. I prayed for a miracle.

But my only response was the hiss of the ventilator pushing air in, and taking it out.

In and out, in and out.

Dr. Walsh walked in and greeted us with a forced smile and her signature sense of calmness that at least gave us assurance that Josiah was in good hands.

"Thanks for being here, Colleen," Jen whispered to Dr. Walsh over the bed.

"Of course," she replied with a soft smile. "How are you guys holding up?"

"We're . . . OK."

As an intern, Dr. Walsh was not allowed to do extra shifts or even overtime, but at the end of her shift, she would always stop and check in, not only on Josiah but also with Jen. She was like an angel sent from God. Her outgoing personality and her caring heart were like a breath of fresh air for all of us.

Dr. Walsh's entire career had been pushing to find clear, definitive, correct answers that helped people. From pushing her brother during his college application process, to choosing to become a pediatric doctor for the very reason to save kids' lives, Dr. Walsh was destined to fight for this little boy's life long before she even knew it.

She spent each night reading every medical journal, studying every medical textbook, and trying with every ounce of energy she had left to understand what was going on in this little boy's body. The more she searched, the less she found, and her new life with her husband slowly vanished. Like all of us, her life was chained to hospital room, and her heart remained with a little boy that just could not get better.

It just didn't make sense. She just couldn't understand how there could be a diagnosis, treatment, and still no sign of improvement. The entire past year, every solution the hospital spit out would only temporarily fix a problem before setting off a new issue, to then handle the new issue, which would set off the next—the cycle snowballed.

She spent more time beside this little boy than most other doctors would even consider, and she still had no answers. With every extra shift, every piece of research, and every moment she spent with Josiah, she found more problems than solutions.

Most nights, the only answers she received were, "Go home, Colleen," from her superior, because pushing beyond thirty-six consecutive hours in a hospital became a legal concern. Like trying to hold two handfuls of sand, the harder she clutched on to saving this little boy, the quicker the sand slipped through her fingers, and all she could do was cry into her husband's arms each night as she watched Josiah get sicker.

All of our lives were wrapped up in that little boy's hospital. Jen and Daisha lived in that room, as if they were two permanent fixtures, along with a little boy whose breaths were pushed and pulled through a machine.

Every time I walked in, my eyes darted around the room checking his vitals, looking for his saturation, anything that my thirty years of EMT senses wanted to reevaluate. It was just a way to keep my mind moving, or at least my way of trying to do my part.

I always came to the hospital prepared. Ever since Josiah was born I did my own research and did my homework. I thought no one would be able to pull one over on me; I would be prepared to give an answer or fire back with a question to protect my little boy the only way I knew how. Most times I would even wear my team-issued EMT shirt to show the medical staff they weren't going to confuse us with the medical jargon, especially those first-year residents. Book smart, but had never actually been around death, and that was something that couldn't be taught in a classroom.

In more than thirty years as an EMT, I had seen a lot of it. Motor vehicle accidents with severe injuries. Decapitated bodies within twisted metal wreckage that was once a car or truck. Suicides with a gun or drugs. Young and old. Dead bodies lying for a week in a home or car. There had been a lot, but the only constant in that line of work was the smell. As soon as you opened a door you knew. The distinct smell of a rotting human body will never leave you.

The first time, it will hang on you for a week. You'll smell it in your clothing, you'll smell it in your car, and you'll smell it in your bed at night—it's in your brain. Then after the second time, maybe only a day or two, and after the third time, it becomes a gauge—your frame of reference—but you will never forget it. I have great respect for anyone who has fought in war, anyone who has had to witness death and live with it day in and day out. There's no smell like that on the entire planet.

Death does not discriminate between nationality, race, gender, or age. Over time, I had built a wall to death. I saw a dead body as a place where someone once lived. Like a home, they leave and the house becomes empty. The person within leaves, but the house remains. Empty. Void of life.

Most want to live. Most fight for it. But there are times when we are the last person they talk to and then they go into cardiac arrest, and ours is the last hand they hold before their body slips way. Some make it, some don't. It's sometimes hard to understand why. But it's not up to us to understand; it's up to us to fight for the lives in front of us. That's why we do what we do. To do our best to give someone a second chance.

Those moments so close to death gave me a deeper appreciation of life and the future's unpredictability. Death had pulled me to areas I never wished to explore, while life had pushed me to heights I had never imagined. The constant tug of life and death had made me conquer fears, find acceptance, and above all, seek God.

But something changes when your own flesh and blood is battling death. It no longer becomes cherishing the balance of existence. It's grabbing the handle of life and pushing for all you're worth. But after the second day of Josiah's coma, I began to realize that no matter how hard we pushed, our only sign of life was the wheezing breath of Josiah's monster.

In and out, in and out.

6

WALLS

IN HIGH SCHOOL, FAMILY meant nothing to me. I built walls around whatever that word meant so I would never need to face that man again. I stopped pulling my hair out and started closing myself off to the world. Spring quickly turned to summer, and as my senior year of high school was rapidly approaching I started walking to the football field to meet up with a few friends. It was our routine; weekends we would backpack through a portion of the PA State Game Lands called Greenland, and during the week we would meet up after class to shoot the breeze. It kept us at bay and kept me out of the house.

After I graduated high school, I was hanging out with my niece at a neighboring school district football field. I had just joined the PA Air National Guard and was waiting to deploy to basic training in Texas. I saw a girl walking across the field and asked my niece who she was. She told me her name was Debra Long. To me she was beautiful and polite, so we did what we were supposed to and started dating. My girlfriend invited me to church on a Wednesday night. *"Wednesday night?"* I thought. *"Who goes to church on a Wednesday night?"* But I went along anyway. That was my first encounter with Jesus Christ.

Now it seemed to all add up.

The small cross that glowed. The one who I would pray to but didn't know who or what He was. That night I asked His forgiveness and accepted Jesus as my Savior. Trumpets didn't play, angels didn't sing, and my problems didn't go away. It almost seemed to agitate my demons, bang their cages, and bring them to battle even more. I didn't realize it then, but I still had a long way to go.

After coming home from basic training, Deb and I got engaged, and a year later we were married. I thought it would be the perfect mix: The military would help channel my anger, and my new branch of the family would let me forget about my previous one. In the beginning, it worked. But then little by little the anger I would release in the military started to seep into our home life. By the time I realized my anger had derailed a new marriage, it was too late. It was sad, really. Neither of us ever knew what a real relationship was supposed to be.

My entire family slipped into the same trap. We all tried to grow up as fast as we could and move on like nothing ever happened. But we all continued the pattern. It was our generational sin, so to speak. My brother had a chance, though. He married a decent woman and got a great career as a foreman in Massachusetts welding oxygen fuel cells for NASA. But he drank himself into oblivion and lost his job. Soon after, his wife divorced him. But I never took a sip. I never drank, never smoked, and never did drugs. I made it out—and didn't know why.

Deb and I would yell, she would scream, and our fights escalated to the point where we wondered why we even got married in the first place. But we were both two kids trying to handle it all.

We fought for superiority; someone had to be right, while the other had to be proven wrong—and we weren't stopping until a verdict was reached. The truth always got lost and we argued just to show who was in charge.

* * *

My mom found Jesus shortly after I did. The day I told her I went to church, she was speechless.

"Dave went to church!? What happened?" She was so curious that she came to church on Sunday and found what she had longed for but didn't understand. That night she asked Jesus into her life. That was in the fall of 1973. Shortly after, and prior to my wedding in 1975, my mom became extremely ill. In 1976, about seven months after our first child, Lisa, was born, my mom passed away with cancer.

I know I will see her again in Heaven.

Within months of my mom's passing, my wife and I separated, and my demons became alive. The arguing, the fighting, the distance we put between each other made us believe we shouldn't have gotten married in the first place. But we made a commitment, a lifelong commitment, and we tried again to make it work. The arguing and fighting continued on and off for years. It affected our family and changed my relationship with my precious daughter Jen in ways I never knew imaginable.

Eventually, Deb, our three teenagers, and I moved into a house in small town called Hegins, Pennsylvania. Built three stories, straight up, the house was small, but it felt big at the same time. It was never my home, though; my sanctuary was running in the back of a volunteer ambulance. It was where I felt most comfortable, and it was where I felt like I could actually make a difference in another person's life. But I was spiritually stagnant. The abuser of my past still haunted me with every step, and as I closed my life off to him, I did the same to my own family. The ambulance became my escape hatch from reality. I was so willing to help others, but I didn't want to deal with my own family issues—or perhaps I just couldn't.

As the years have passed since my first call as an EMT, I'm not sure if I'd grown callus to it, or simply built walls to block the emotion. The only way I could separate the joy of life from the hurt I experienced was in the back of an ambulance. As the call comes in, we head out; and the race for life begins. Some fear death; some hate it. But for me, I've had to respect it, and learned to understand it. Thirty years as an EMT have forced me to be trapped within the struggle between life and death. It's unpredictable, and when I perform CPR I don't know if that person will make it or not; I am focused on trying to give them another breath and another chance.

It is tough to understand that death is out of our control while someone's final moments remain in our hands. But in the darkest hour, seeing a person survive and have another chance at life is the reason for our work. Though when our efforts fall short and death takes another, I have to look at that person as if their spirit just left us. I guess it's my way of dealing with it—I tell myself the person is just no longer here—this is just the space on earth they used to occupy, and this is just a building they used to live within. Death has simply pulled the spirit away.

I separate and build yet another wall.

But that's how I have dealt with everything in my life.

I found ways to separate, to hide from what I didn't want to face, and told myself to just run away. I guess that was why my office, and the countless nights I spent huddled around a CB radio, felt more like home than my house ever did. My home was at the station.

My temper grew. I lived by the force that saved me from my childhood attacker and that became the model for my parenting. I would yell and scream, so our kids listened by fear. I would think it was OK. It was discipline, structure. I would rationalize, and it was the only way I could prove a point.

I pushed my kids away. I gave them every reason to move as soon as they could, and I saw myself become the man I hated most. It felt like every time I made a vow to change, I would fall into the same pattern, building a wall between my family and myself, higher than it had ever been before.

The moment my family huddled around a silent hospital bed, I knew they deserved better.

*   *   *

While Josiah was in Children's Two, I did everything to make sure our family was happy, stable, and living life with the love a family should have. That floor became our home. Even the halls were more like a neighborhood than a hospital. The nurses' circulation table still held the same buzz as a town square, and the nurses felt more like extended family than practitioners. Family memories were created and memorialized all within that floor—the elevator where we lost Daisha, the play area where we attempted to have "family time," the elevator where we found Daisha, and the rooms where Josiah spent his life became our landmarks.

But the longer Josiah was in Children's Two, the more the medical team couldn't get enough of him. Naturally, his unique case brings in the initial attraction, but there's something about his smile that makes people want to find out more. Time and time again, nurses and doctors kept commenting on his irresistible grin, but nurse Kim was so taken by our little boy's smile, she couldn't stop coming into room. As tough as the days were, every moment Kim and Josiah were together, the playful spirit of the floor came to life, and we got to see the joy of God placed in both of their hearts. Children's Two felt like home to Josiah, and Kim made sure of that.

Before the surgery that sent Josiah into his coma, I visited the hospital room pulling a red wagon. It was just a red and black plastic wagon with an IV stand in the back, but it was something Josiah and Daisha looked forward to and it meant family time.

Daisha and I pulled up to his room, and you could see the smile on Josiah's face from down the hall. He knew it was time for our nightly ride, and all three of us felt the same joy that shone through that little boy's smile. The nurses helped string his IV and lowered Josiah onto Daisha's lap, and then we were off.

I pulled them down the hallway, turned around, and then went back the other way toward the elevators, down to the lobby, and around and around we would go. I looked back, and like usual they were about to fall asleep. Daisha would always doze off first—I think Josiah was too excited to be out of his room.

But every time I pulled that wagon I felt like I was at peace. I may not have been much of a dad, but I vowed that I'd be a better grandfather. For the first time, I held my family in my arms like I never have before, and I felt God do the same within me.

In those moments, we were surrounded by the peace God gave us in the hospital, and I felt the love and joy that being a grandparent should always yield.

We were together. We were one. And even under the worst and most horrid conditions, we were a family.

The time in the hospital forced Jen and I to work with each other, and even though our problems were not solved, we had a place in each other's lives—and that was a start.

We would journey through the hospital and complete our loop time and time again. Sometimes we would walk for hours pretending we were on an exotic safari together in the jungle, or sometimes the exploration was filled with the sleeping silence of two little ones.

7

COMA: PART 3

THE WEEK CONTINUED AND Josiah showed no signs of improvement. They couldn't flush the infection anymore because it only increased with the hour and now his only functional lung was weakening. His health was fading fast. With each minimal breath, Josiah struggled to breathe and continued fighting an unwinnable battle. As quickly as the ventilator filled his lung, the oxygen escaped and the wheezing of the ventilator resonated throughout the room.

In and out, in and out.

Our good friend Kimmie and the other nurses from Children's Two came by the first day of his coma, but today she was alone. Their unit had been talking about Josiah—and how much time he had left—and she needed to see him. She walked in and saw us like she had many times before: exhausted and emotionally drained. She held Jen and me hovering around Josiah's bed, and I knew Kimmy could feel us both silently crying. Our red eyes and staggered breaths told Kimmie all she needed to know, then she looked over and saw Josiah.

The child she fell in love with the moment he entered Children's Two, her partner in crime, and the brightest smile on the floor was now a lifeless body connected to a ventilator. She began to cry as her fingertips gently grazed over Josiah's forehead, but the hand that once tickled down Josiah's body eliciting a flood of laughter and smiles was now still and the body now cold. Tears ran down her cheeks as she realized this was no longer the same child that entered Children's Two—her little buddy was all but gone.

No words could comfort; no touch could heal.

Everyone in the hospital felt a connection with Jo, and everyone pushed in his fight for life. But it wasn't just about Josiah's medical care. Our family spent so much time in the hospital; the staff began to take care of all of us. Daisha spent most of her toddler years roaming the halls and finding ways to explore every inch of the hospital. She has always been a fearless older sister. From sleeping next to Josiah's bedside and loving her family to no end, Daisha could always put a smile on our faces. And to this day, we are told the reason for the security cameras on the elevators is from the time Daisha decided to wander through the biggest hospital in the eastern United States.

By the time Josiah was twelve months, we'd spent nearly his whole life in the hospital. Just like so many times before, we sat in his room chatting with the nurses and doctors. As they began to make their rounds, my daughter and I decided to grab a cup of coffee but could not find Daisha. The pediatric center had plenty of play areas meant to distract young family members from the reason they came to a hospital, so we figured Daisha was mesmerized by the life-sized teddy bears and had just wandered off. We searched and searched, but she was nowhere to be found. As we kept looking, nurses joined us, then the doctors, and then everyone on hospital floor began looking for this sweet little girl.

We checked in every room, under every desk, on every table, and in every seat, but no luck. My daughter began to worry, but just as we were desperately trying to figure out what to do, the elevator dinged. We ran over to the opening doors, and there stood a nurse and Daisha jumping around with the biggest smile on her face. The nurse found Daisha at her favorite place in the hospital, the "Turtle Fountain" at the main entrance. We should have guessed.

As much as I fought going to Children's Two and having our little boy live in the hospital, I would trade anything to be back in room 282 instead of where we were now.

* * *

The morning came after another night of sleeping in the hospital, and our routine started again. The medical staff sat down with a box of tissues, reviewing the same coma, talking about the same issues, and then mentioned what everyone had been avoiding: turning off his ventilator.

Dr. Walsh was always the first one to sit with us and the last one to leave us. We knew the pain running through our bodies was shared, and the moment she started speaking, we could see her fight back tears.

"He's fought a good fight," she began. "But the infection is quickly shutting down his body. There is just nothing more we can do."

The room fell silent and the monster pushing Josiah's breaths got louder.

In and out, in and out.

The medical staff had nothing else to say. Josiah was out of options, and now out of time. They came over to us and we crumbled in their arms. Jen and I held them, they held us, and we held each other.

In and out, in and out.

Josiah was dying.

No matter how hard we pushed or what treatment the staff tried, his health was a series of fires, and as hard as the medical staff fought, it kept building until the entire forest was going up in flames.

Nothing else could be done.

But to wrestle with the idea of shutting off your grandson's ventilator is something I wish no family would ever have to decide. The thought of our own little boy being brought into this world only to be taken away haunted me to no end. But at what point was our desire to wield Josiah to health becoming a burden of pain put on a child? At what point did our obsession to prolong his life make him suffer a painful death?

The room filled with tears, and our fragmented conversation continued.

"There has to be something that will give him more time, right?" Jen pleaded through a wave of tears.

"Josiah is barley holding on. We just don't have anything else to give him," a doctor whispered as delicately as possible.

Our conversation stopped; the only voice that continued was Josiah's monster alone. Heavy sobs were the only rebuttal to the reality we faced. We were alone, and in that room, we were dead. *In and out, in and out.*

*   *   *

I tried to clear my mind and stepped outside for a minute. I walked back to the fuzzy bear painting and tasted the final memory we had of Josiah's life. He was such a happy kid and now I didn't know what we had left. I turned back from my walk, but as I left the hallway I was drawn to a window; not a pane to the outside world but a window of confinement, a glimpse of another world trapped inside of ours—a fish tank in the play area.

Maybe it was a moment of weakness, or just the shimmering light that caught my wandering eyes, but I caught a look at the fish swimming around a sunken pirate ship and joked to myself about how much these fish must be wishing their pirate ship didn't have cannon holes in the sides so it could sail them back to sea. But as I looked at the fish and joked about their predicament, the light broke through the second pane and I was no longer looking at a fish tank but rather a mirror. It sunk in that the person staring back at me was thinking the same thing about my own life.

The restart to our lives was supposed to be liberating and not imprisoning. It was all supposed to be over. My constricting childhood, suffocating my existence to the point of never knowing how to function in the world, was supposed to be settled. My own family—deprived and hurt, never knowing a life other than the hell I gave them—was supposed to restart with love. And now Josiah—trapped and dying with no way out—was supposed to be a healthy, happy baby boy. We were supposed to swim free from the misery of our lives, but when the light finally subsided and I saw the fish swimming around the broken pirate ship, I was no longer looking at the ones held captive—they were.

*   *   *

We started a routine. In the morning, Colleen and the rest of the staff entered the room with a box of tissues and explained to us that Josiah's health was deteriorating with no signs of improvement. We talked about a timeline, options, and how much longer Josiah could fight.

Then we would cry.

"Josiah is still unresponsive," the doctors told us. "I'm sorry, we can't do anything else."

They told us what we already knew. But we needed their honesty. We needed their abrupt dose of reality because as much as we wanted Josiah to fight—as much as we *needed* Josiah to fight—he was suffering and so were we. We knew Josiah was unresponsive, we knew he was dying, but what we didn't know was when.

"We can see if he improves tonight," Jen would plead, wiping away her tears.

"Of course."

As the medical staff left, Colleen would stay with us and we would mourn. Sometimes we would cry together or sometimes we would sit in silence, feeling the jagged ends of pain cutting through our hearts in ways we would only know, but we sat together and shared its burden.

Then, as the morning turned to day and day turned to night, I would sit next to Josiah and sing "If I Could Just Sit With You Awhile," by Dennis Jernigan. The song had been used as part of our church's Easter Day play, which my son produced, and the moment I heard it, it grabbed me. Every moment in that hospital room that I was weak, and my faith succumbed to despair, that tune swirled around my head and I could not shake the lyrics.

> When I cannot feel
> When my wounds don't heal
> Lord I humbly kneel
> Hidden in you*

Pain is all we ever knew. Our family, this coma, and the lifetime before this, cut us and damaged us like wounds that we couldn't

---

heal. The pain I felt as a child resurfaced, and as I touched my little man I thought of the childhood taken from me, the childhood I took from my children, the life that was being taken from Josiah, and I thought of who saved me.

What I couldn't feel at the time of my greatest pain was that someone cared for me. Someone loved me. Someone saved me.

My neighbor, Margie. Our Sunday school teacher and piano player, never married.

She held me in her arms and would sing the most beautiful hymns as I fell asleep. Admittedly it was one of the reasons why I felt like I needed to sing to Josiah. Maybe in some way, the song Margie sang over me gave a shield no abuser could break, and childishly I thought maybe mine could do the same.

She had no idea what I went through or what that man was doing to us as children, but Margie held my innocence like a rare treasure. She gave me the love I needed, the love I deserved. The seeds of grace were planted in my heart, and after decades of growing and maturing, her love allowed the seed to take root years later in the soil that I believed was dead.

And Josiah's life was no different. In Romans 5:3-5, Paul says, "We can rejoice, too, when we run into problems and trials, for we know that they help us develop endurance. And endurance develops strength of character, and character strengthens our confident hope of salvation."

Sometimes we cry out and think God doesn't hear us and ask why us, or why Josiah. But we learned our strength comes from our moments of weakness, and our bravery comes from the battles in which we are matched. And from the time Josiah was born, God created him to take root, to stand tall in the face of evil, and endure.

Things happen that oftentimes get our attention. People, situations, or events tend to strengthen our faith, and in many times, adversity draws us closer to Him. As people, we often forget that we are God's children. We want to grab life by our own handles and push in the direction we want, but the road to salvation has no shortcuts, and with each trial we face, our faith grows.

I continued to sing, and my journey in faith continued to take root. Maybe I was still searching. Searching for answers, wondering why or how we got to this point, or how a family sitting so close to each other could feel so distant, or how the beginning of a boy's life could feel so close to its end. But the moments in song made us feel alive and gave us the intimate moments with God that we needed.

> If I could just sit with you awhile
> If you could just hold me
> Nothing could touch me
> Though I'm wounded
> Though I die*

As those lyrics came off my tongue, I knew we were in God's presence. Even though Josiah was unconscious I believed he could hear me singing. I guess it was my way of encouraging not only him, but me as well.

I've always known Josiah has a unique relationship with God that I could never quite understand, but as I sang those words, something inside of me knew that God had Josiah exactly where he wanted him. It was subtle, and most of the time felt too distant to hold, but I believe that's where you find your true grace. Not in the moment where you feel like you have achieved God's favor, but in the times you feel like God is nowhere to be found and you reach for God anyway.

A nurse making her rounds heard my song and gazed through the doorway. I finished the final note and looked over at her in the entryway. Leaning on the wall with hands over her face and tears in her eyes, she looked at me and said, "Don't give up on this little boy. God's not done with him yet."

8

THE FINAL DIAGNOSIS

AT BIRTH, JOSIAH LOOKED like a healthy baby boy. On May 25, 2004, we couldn't have been happier to welcome the newest member of our family to the world.

But over the next few weeks, we noticed Josiah's skin was very red and looked somewhat like a premature baby. This wasn't too alarming, as we believed it would gradually change over time, but we had no idea how severe this would become.

* * *

I was spending another long day at work and was preparing my mind to spend another shift with the ambulance when my cell phone rang. It was Jen.

"I can't feed him," Jen cried as we talked on the phone. "Every time we try to feed him he just spits it back up."

"He did the same yesterday," I replied, accidentally stating the obvious.

"I know, it's been like this for a few days. Let's get an appointment and take him to our pediatrician Dr. Geafania."

We knew there had to be some explanation. Maybe it was the formula. Maybe he had the stomach bug. Whatever the case, we would find the reason and our lives would be back to normal.

* * *

DR. COLLEEN WALSH

In his first few weeks, Josiah gained very little weight, if any. Doctor G, as the family called him, tried everything: new diets, new formulas, new ideas, which only deepened the confusion. He didn't know what was wrong, so he recommended a rheumatologist.

Josiah was sent to Janet Weis Children's Hospital as part of Geisinger Medical Center in Danville, Pennsylvania, one of the most advanced hospitals in the eastern United States. It gave the family their first true hope in healing Josiah. Healing: a word which at the time they thought to be the goal, a word they thought could be obtained, but became a word that would soon mean so little.

They drove through the campus of Geisinger to find the right building of a hospital that seemed to never end. Buildings piled on top of buildings and black asphalt painted a mountainside barely able to hold all of its occupants.

They met with the rheumatologist, and even he was at a loss. So after a short visit, Josiah was sent to a pediatric dermatologist.

But they didn't just meet one specialist. The confusing and ambiguous case of this little boy spread, and Geisinger enlisted a team of their best and brightest doctors.

Within the small army of medical professionals running in and out of the room was a resident, Dr. Colleen Walsh. Fresh out of completing her pediatric internship at Geisinger, Dr. Walsh joined the hospital residency in June—one month after Josiah was born—and became a familiar face by Josiah's bedside. She added extra shifts to her already overworked and understaffed residency program just to be with Josiah on her much-needed nights off (and a few years later, even did her final presentation to complete her residency on Josiah). She took on his disease not just as a medical enigma, but as a personal mission to heal this little boy.

It was no surprise that Dr. Walsh dove right into this peculiar case. Growing up in North Hampton, Pennsylvania, Colleen knew she was going to be a doctor since the fifth grade. Smart, driven, and the type of perfectionist that would condemn the world if a "C" had shown on her transcript, she was never afraid to push until she found the correct answer—no matter what.

Admittedly, when her video-game-addict, book-hating little brother mentioned that he might not go to college, Colleen, the already full-time field hockey player and Dean's List pre-med and biology major at Moravian College, did not like that answer one bit and would not accept it.

So she pushed him; well, she hounded him.

Arbitrary college information sessions, future major ideas, even forcing him on a college visit to Moravian, became a weekly obsession. Maybe it worked, and he gained a new perspective, or maybe it was to end her sheer torture, but the next year he left for college. Four years later he was accepted into graduate school and today currently has a master's degree working for a company developing the latest technology for—how fitting—video games.

The moment she laid eyes on Josiah, she brought that same relentless conviction. The fact that this little boy just couldn't be fed was unacceptable to her, and like everything she encountered, she was going to find the answer she wanted.

*   *   *

When we first walked into Geisinger it was a blur. A blur of doctors, specialists, surgeons, and second and third opinions shuffled in and out of the room, while we sat and waited as this peculiar case seemed to find more questions than answers.

So we sat by Josiah's bedside, answering every question from the army of doctors without finding any answer in return. But most nights, after all the residents left, Dr. Colleen Walsh would step in as a new friend—and a new hope—and began to flourish.

In the early summer of 2004, Josiah was admitted to room 282 of Geisinger's Children's Hospital 2nd floor, or Children's Two, and there was no change in his health. His redness remained, and he still couldn't keep any formula down, no matter what experiment they tried. Wires and tubes connected to every monitor in the room coiled around his body like snakes while confusion circled his bed to match.

There were no answers; only seemingly repeated questions from the rapid visits of doctors in an out of the room, each finding the same inevitable frustration as the last. Time at his bedside stood still, and like the best and brightest doctors they had to work on his case, we were at a loss. I think it was more of a shock to see our boy lie in a hospital bed rather than our own home.

Everything became real.

Time, family, and healing: all three words slowly drifted away as we watched our little boy being connected to tubes and wires. I don't know how Jen did it. Sleeping next to her son in the hospital every night of the week, you could see she was exhausted. But every time Josiah's eyes opened, so did her own, and she made sure to bring the biggest smile on her little boy's face. He was only a baby—too young to know where he was but old enough to know he didn't want to be there—and Jen made sure to be fighting alongside him.

* * *

We walked into the room, and I knew it wouldn't be a pleasant visit. We were in dermatology, an unfamiliar section of the hospital, and I could sense something was just not right. The dermatologist examined Josiah's medical history, which was rapidly becoming as thick as a novel. He glanced over Josiah's arms and legs, examining the skin in full detail and then flipped back through his medical pages again. There was an uneasy feeling that he was looking for something, and as my heart began to pound, I sank into my chair.

He was only four weeks old and hadn't gained a pound. No one knew why our little boy seemed to fall sicker each day, but the dermatologist told us Josiah possibly had "stiff skin syndrome" which is a rare disorder that causes the skin to tighten all over a person's body. It still didn't explain the weight loss or vomiting, but the idea fit their guidelines and had to be tested.

The doctor explained the procedure and my heart sank. The bad feeling walking into the patient room turned another knot in my stomach. He detailed the test, and it required a skin sample or punch biopsy. This is usually once a local anesthetic is injected, a small cookie cutter punch is pushed down and rotated into the skin to remove the desired sample.

Usually.

But Josiah was not strong enough for the anesthetic.

This must be a modified test, I kept reasoning with myself. *There'll be another way.* But my chest tightened when he said they needed to retain the sample. *They have a plan. They're gonna take care of it.* I desperately tried to believe they wouldn't consider putting a four-week-old boy through such agony but also knew they needed the sample.

I held Josiah and prayed over him. The doctor cleaned the specialty instrument and disinfected Josiah's leg. I took a deep breath. *God protect him, God protect him, God, please protect him, please God protect him, please God protect please protect him.* My heart was racing and I could feel the knot in my stomach tightening. *They can't be doing this. This won't happen.* But with one swift motion, the dermatologist pushed the blade deep into Josiah's skin, and he let out the most horrific scream. The sound that exited our little boy's body is something I will never forget. Josiah screamed on the table and his cry pierced through the room. The doctor twisted the circular instrument then drew the blade out from the skin leaving a circle of blood at the base of Josiah's muscle. I tried to console him as the dermatologist calmly placed the sample in a medical kit to be sent for testing, but it was no use. It took about fifteen minutes to calm him.

His screams echoed in my head, and his pain became real. The confusion throughout his short life thus far, the unknowns doctors tried to quantify, and the desperation we felt in our hearts, led to more unanswered questions.

I understood they needed the sample and I understood the test was necessary, but it was the worst day we ever had. Or so we thought. Our family was about to undergo another stressful event that would test the resolve of us all.

* * *

Pain was all this little boy had known, but God made him stronger than we had ever imagined. Each time I thought about the day of Josiah's skin sample, I thought about the Old Testament story of Job. Job was an innocent man who suffered terribly by the will of the Lord. He was one of God's most faithful followers, and as a challenge to his faith, he was stripped of his riches, health, and loved ones.

In the last trial, the Devil took Job's farm, his family, and branded him with nasty blisters and boils all over his body. Job was so weak; all he could do was lie on the floor and scream in pain to the Lord. But as his body withered and his spirit was tested, his faith remained. God rewarded Job by blessing him with ten times more than he previously had and was eternally praised by the Lord.

As I thought about Job, I thought about Josiah. Seeing our boy lying on the table screaming in pain—almost as his cry to God—I couldn't help but think he would be rewarded. Pain may have brought Josiah into this world, but I knew his toughness and God's love would bring him life.

It had to.

There was no other choice.

* * *

From the very beginning, there was another doctor who fought alongside Josiah: Dr. Cochran, a pediatric gastroenterologist. With all the feeding issues that Josiah was having, he was the one who did everything he could to help Josiah thrive. But, through no fault of his own, everything he tried was to no avail. We didn't know at the time that Josiah had an intestinal birth defect that was shutting down his ability to thrive. Dr. Cochran was the one who sent Josiah to CHOP. He told Jen, "We need another set of eyes. I just don't know what is happening. Maybe someone there can help us."

During the first several months of Josiah's life, there was another battle being fought that would further test our resolve. My wife, Deb—or "Nana," as Josiah and Daisha called her—spent months fighting an infection in her foot due to diabetes. We were dealing with sickness now on two fronts. During that time, there were many doctor and hospital visits for not only Josiah but also his Nana. But Deb was the prayer warrior, the one quietly behind the scenes praying for Josiah. Even though she was dealing with a severe infection in her foot, and later it spreading to her leg, she was always along on Josiah's doctor visits helping take care of Daisha when Josiah was in and out of the hospital. In March of 2005, Deb had her right leg amputated. She continued as best she could to help, vigilantly praying for this little boy. Never underestimate the power of prayer by mothers and grandmothers. Sometimes on this earth, they are the forgotten warriors—but not forgotten by God.

We celebrated Josiah's first birthday like any other toddler's: cake, candles, celebratory cone hats, presents, and a family gathered around a hospital bed singing to their little boy. The medical staff sang along too, as they were our closest friends for the past year, and we tried to spend one day laughing and celebrating to escape the uneasiness that weighed on us all.

After our little birthday escape and a number of dead-end theories from the medical staff, Dr. Cochran decided it was in Josiah's best interest to send him to CHOP, Children's Hospital of Philadelphia. It's the nation's top children's hospital and regularly flies in the world's most complex cases, and we were just a three-hour drive away. In relativity, the short distance was a real blessing, but we didn't realize this was the nation's top hospital or that it was Geisinger's SOS call in solving Josiah's puzzling illness. And we didn't know this was our last and only chance at a true diagnosis.

I was working the day shift at the time and couldn't make the trip because most of my vacation and sick days were already gone from all the days I called off in the past year. So this was a solo journey for Jen. We had found ways to work together. I had to work to keep our house afloat, so she would handle the checkups—not only for Josiah, but also for Nana—while I was at the factory. We worked together as best we could at taking care of Josiah and Nana.

In the morning, Jen and Josiah were sent to CHOP, and I headed in for work. That night, I headed home from the welding plant as the orange sky fell behind the mountains. The moment I sat down at the kitchen table, my phone buzzed. I looked at my cell phone dancing on top of the surface, lighting the slowly dimming room, and I swallowed hard.

It was Jen.

I quickly flipped open my phone and pressed it to my ear.

"Dad?" She said panting.

"Yeah, honey?"

"It's bad. Real bad."

I hung up the phone after Jen told me the diagnosis and sat there and just stared at the kitchen table. I felt numb. I guess deep down we wanted to know the battle we had to face, but there was no fighting this one.

The health care system's flying darts fell on the disturbing genetic disorder of Hutchinson-Guilford Progeria Syndrome. It's an incurable genetic disease that causes rapid aging in children, about ten years for every one year of life, making a life expectancy of thirteen to eighteen years old.

Hutchinson-Guilford Progeria Syndrome or simply, Progeria, is so rare that only one in four million births have a reported incidence of the disease. Currently, there are 112 children world-wide diagnosed with HGPS, and approximately sixteen live in the United States. It's a devastating disease that pulls life away from the victim in clear daylight. As Josiah grew, the disease became visible, and all we could do was watch as his body started to age and steadily decline.

Year by year, the body weakens, slow enough that you don't even notice it, but just quick enough that you recall the strength he once had. If a person's life is not cut short by accident or ill-ness, we all grow old. Our bodies' vital functions start to deterio-rate with time. For children with HGPS, this happens much more rapidly. It's a cruel disease not only for the victims, but also for the families and all those who have become close friends.

There were no more hospitals, no other referral, and no magic wish. Just the harsh reality of a terminally ill little boy.

Progeria is so rare that at the time of Josiah's diagnosis, it wasn't even studied at every medical school. The doctors ordered x-rays of his ribs and hands and then ordered genetic testing to find out if the peculiar case of Progeria was finally the right diagnosis.

That night, as the hospital tucked in and Josiah fell soundly asleep in a new hospital bed that had been all too familiar, Jen went for a walk. She needed to see it for herself and as she walked the dark hallways of an empty hospital, she found the glow of a computer screen and sat down.

She needed an answer.

She was supposed to be home, raising a family growing up slow in the Pennsylvania hills. Not spending an entire childhood at another hospital and another night spent on the pleather couch of her child's room. The months of confusion had stolen every precious moment away from her little boy, and with each day he grew weaker. The questions behind this little boy's health became overwhelming, and she needed an answer—we all needed an answer.

She stared at the computer screen as her fingers pecked at the keyboard.

She pressed ENTER, and by the time the key rose back to the keyboard, there was Josiah's face.

It was him.

His every feature, his every look, and his every symptom. She finally saw Progeria, and she finally saw Josiah.

Jen and Josiah were transported back to Janet Weis Children's Hospital and the pediatric dermatologist stopped in to check on Josiah while they waited on test results. Jen told him of the diagnosis, and upon hearing the word "Progeria," he stated, "I bet my entire career this is not what Josiah has!"

But within a few weeks the final test results confirmed that Josiah had Hutchinson-Guilford Progeria.

It was final.

Josiah was terminal.

9

COMA: PART 4

JEN AND I SAT with Josiah and just listened to the ventilator hum: *in and out, in and out.* We didn't know what to say or what to do, so we just sat there and listened. I would try to pray but words were tough; we just sat and waited.

I glanced around the room, checking Josiah and hoping for a minor deviation. Heart rate stable; blood pressure 138/52. No change. I checked again. No change. No matter how many times I hunted for a variation, something to keep me preoccupied other than my own grandson drifting away before my eyes, I only found the answers I wasn't looking for.

Each time I checked Josiah, I was drawn to the window. I looked out and saw the picturesque mountainside surrounding the hospital—mesmerizing enough to forget where I was for a moment and lovely enough to justify thanking God for the beauty. I studied her ridges and the walloping blotches of orange and crimson gradually overtaking the lush green as summer faded to fall. I imagined our home behind those hills and thought about the trip through each of the dips and turns we took to get here. I followed the curves until the mountainside stretched beyond my range of perception and looked like the foggy background to an oil painting of the sun slowly fading into a horizon.

That view was my sanctuary at the station. Every summer night I would peek through my office window and watch the burnt orange sun sink below the tree line and light the sky one more time before darkness.

In that moment, I was at peace.

No matter how hard a day at the station was, or how separated our house became, that view was my escape. It reconnected me to the beauty of our world and showed me how insignificant we really are. But beauty isn't realizing our insignificance; it's realizing the peace beyond it. Perhaps the peace we find listening to the birds sing their final song at sunset and watching the last ray of sunlight run across the sky isn't found within ourselves, but realizing the peace we look for is something much bigger than we can ever imagine, and we thank God for giving it to us.

But staring through the windowpane at the Pediatric Intensive Care Unit at the same tree line was no longer my escape. It was a disturbing abyss.

I saw our insignificance next to the vast tree line but saw the peace we were searching for somewhere within a maze Josiah had been journeying through. As we searched day and night, we walked in circles, only finding dead-end paths until there was no other direction to walk.

I saw the mountains, rolling through the beauty God created and couldn't help but feel weak and powerless in comparison. We were stuck gazing at a beauty hidden from our perception, and I couldn't help but wonder if Josiah would ever see the beauty beyond that plastic windowpane or if my view from the PICU window was the final view of the world as he knew it.

Perhaps the reason he was holding on was to find that peace beyond the window, to see the beauty of a sunrise only God can give. Or maybe he was already beyond the windowpane; lost and forgotten like a wounded deer settling down deep in the bush for its final sunset and final night's rest.

I tried to stop looking at the mountain range because what used to give me a true sense of peace in my heart now frightened me to my core. But no matter how much I tried to look away from that window, I kept wondering if Josiah would ever escape this—or if our family ever would either.

* * *

Dr. Walsh walked in and greeted us with a smile, and most importantly, a calmness that gave our hearts assurance that we knew Josiah was in the best care possible.

"Thanks for being here, Colleen," Jen whispered to Dr. Walsh over the bed.

"Of course," she replied with a soft smile. "How are you guys holding up?"

"We're . . . OK."

The coma that seemed to never end turned black and charged through the night. As her shift since last evening was finally about to end, Dr. Walsh prepared to spend yet another night by his bedside. She plugged her stethoscope into her ears to give Josiah one final check before she could spend time with us, but the moment the stethoscope touched his chest, her face dropped.

She checked the right, and then the left. Then the right again. The left again. Dr. Walsh had discovered that Josiah's right lung had completely filled with fluid.

She checked the left again before quickly grabbing a suctioning device while calling the nursing staff into the room. Through Josiah's breathing tube, Dr. Walsh vacuumed out a large amount of fluid, indicating Josiah had gone from bad to worse.

Emotionally drained, and barely accepting the results herself, Dr. Walsh tried to break the news to us that Josiah may not be able to breathe. She didn't have the willpower to sugar coat another bad diagnosis so she gave it to us straight: "With the antibiotics and anti-fungal medication, he's beginning to stabilize for now, but the fluid will have to be suctioned every fifteen minutes and looks like it will increase over time. I'm so sorry, the infection is spreading quicker than we thought."

A fungus had grown on the upper part of his lung and now fluid was pouring in. Dr. Walsh had immediately started to treat him with the prescribed anti-fungal medicine, but the fluid only increased.

Josiah just couldn't catch a break.

Every fifteen minutes, nurses would drain his lung. The fluid was pouring in so quickly that if they missed even one cycle of draining, our little boy would have most likely have died from an effect similar to drowning.

We sank lower into the pleather bench, now realizing the five-day estimate on Josiah's life might only be a wish. The room was

still. Words had escaped us for days but now language seemed to
be a distant memory that we all longed to find. Without a word,
Dr. Walsh touched Josiah's forehead and without fighting for an
extra shift, or staying by his bedside for the evening, she left the
room and walked out of the hospital for the night.

*   *   *

DR. COLLEEN WALSH

A silent car ride brought her to her house. Mindlessly turning off her car and
walking through the door, Colleen sobbed. Tears poured down her face as she
fell into her husband John's arms. The pain she had been holding back finally
broke like the snap of a levy, and she collapsed into her husband's embrace,
the only thing stopping her from crumbling to their bedroom floor.

She had cried before, but never like this.

Every day she picked herself up off the ground and put on an armor of
strength for the family. She'd come home, fall apart, and do it again the
next day. She didn't want Josiah to see her in any other way. He didn't need
another reason to die, nor did she want to give the family another reason to
give up faith.

So she fought for Josiah and was the epitome of selflessness. But that
night, she was done.

For eleven months, she had been trying to hold it together. Eleven months
she had fought to find a solution. And for eleven months, she had believed
there was one.

But this time, she saw the end.

Josiah was out of options. The fight was lost and hope was gone.

"That's it, John," she sobbed, "That's it. It's over, John. It's all over."

*   *   *

In and out, in and out.

*   *   *

Holding our little boy made the decision even harder. We
wanted him to keep fighting but didn't know how much he had
left.

I sat next to him and cried for longer than I can remember. It could have been an hour, or three, or maybe the whole morning, but time was irrelevant; the only time we thought about was how much Josiah had left.

Then it began to sink in.

This was it.

Leaning over a hospital bed hopelessly talking to our little boy became all too familiar. The days ran together as our routine became numbing. I looked around the room absorbing everything it had offered to us for so long and realized the hospital room had consumed me. The discomfort of a pleather hospital chair; the unsettling warmth of the masked scent of sickness; the cheap, uniform beige paint job on the walls; and the sight of my daughter weeping with the tormenting view of the mountain range became images burned into my memory. We prayed and hugged and sang and tried to avoid the inevitable, but our routine had begun and our options were ending.

Josiah was in pain and so were we.

Jen made the heart-wrenching decision to turn off his ventilator the next day.

Hope was gone, but surprisingly, faith remained. Most people can't comprehend having faith after our grandson now had a death date, but it wasn't just faith in what we wanted, it was faith in knowing whatever would be shown to us the next day, we would endure—and so would Josiah, in this world or the next.

It may have seemed fake or fabricated, and maybe for a time it was. But faith is not using God when we feel it's necessary; faith is rooted in the conviction that God is more powerful than we can ever imagine. Faith can and undoubtedly *will* move mountains, but until we can declare that God's love and God's plan for us is greater than our own, our prayers will forever fall short. God is all we ever need, and by the certainty of our faith, God's will has no boundaries.

I prayed, "If you want him now, take him. But I know You are far greater than anything this world can throw at us." Even though we had given up the idea of hope, and my worldly emotions had constantly pushed me in and out of my walk in faith, I finally knew God would take care of everything we needed—including a miracle.

* * *

I tried to escape the closing walls by going on another walk around the hospital for a temporary fix. My walks became known around the hospital—a habit I had formed from my nightly Children's Two routine with Daisha and Josiah in the wagon.

I walked alone and tried to find the solace I was searching for, but my eyes were drawn back to the scuffed tile. The scars, the hurt, the families that had been damaged and glanced over like their existence never mattered, and I couldn't help but think we were now the next scuff to get run over and be slowly forgotten.

I was stopped by almost every worker on the floor wondering if I was looking for someone. I politely told them I was not and I continued my walk; but I guess I was. Perhaps I was looking for someone to lead me away from the hell we were in. Maybe Colleen, Dr. Scorpio, or some other new doctor would magically have just enough time to discover just the right medicine to end this coma and give my little man the life he deserved. But ultimately, I wasn't looking for any of that—I was looking for peace.

The bright windows and open doors of the PICU gave my eyes a personal invitation to a family's most intimate moments. I saw their lives abruptly come to a halt and I witnessed the moment when the possibility of death revealed itself. I watched as families entered a new beginning. Whoever they were before walking through those rattling metal doors had completely been changed, and ready or not, they were entering a life they never knew existed.

I looked into their rooms and I saw Josiah: his past life, our past homes, his fight, and his pain. But the emptiness we had been holding was now unwillingly adopted by the new families that filled each room.

My heart felt what their eyes discovered, and the depth of hurt they were welcomed with was now a life we forever shared. We fought the same battle, searching for optimism while understanding the possibility of a glaring reality, and it's a fight no family should have to lose. But this was also no place a child should be. It's a life no one deserves, but I guess we were all just sentenced to a life we should not have.

As I continued to walk, I saw the same families that were facing the worst pain they never imagined, courageously standing tall and flooding their rooms with affection.

There were kisses sweeter at a hospital bedside than at any honeymoon, hugs tighter at the PICU doorway than any family holiday, and more faith by an IV drip than any church sermon. The floor was filled with death, but it was undoubtedly trumped by love.

It was something I had never seen. It was strength forged through such hardship and a love radiating through such sorrow that it was more than what I believed was humanly possible. It was God's love, and it was the lesson I almost missed. I looked through each door and saw the same families entering their new life with love in their hearts and family by their sides. They were faced with hell but only choosing heaven. It was a world I never knew existed outside of our own, and as I got back to our room, I looked at our child.

I saw a family.

I saw love.

I saw God.

10

THE END

THE INEVITABLE DAY CAME to turn off his ventilator. We walked into the room, and Josiah was still lying there as weak as the day before with a stomach infection as toxic as the day before that, and it seemed only fitting that raindrops began pelting the window, as if the whole world had come to mourn the death of this little boy.

What could you say to a mother the day her son is taken from her? We wanted to comfort Jen, or at least let her know that we love her and would remain at her side, but words never came. We all knew that our love would never fill the void of her own son being ripped away by her own hand. We tried to love her, we tried to be a family, we tried to remain strong, but today our world was about to stop. We tried to prepare for the day that would change us forever.

The PICU doctor came in to talk with Jen. His jaw remained firm, his eyes remained hard, and he looked at Jen and said turning off the ventilator was the only decent option for Josiah. We tried all we could, but like everyone else, we were out of options. He explained that suctioning Josiah's lungs every few minutes and pumping a child full of morphine was no reasonable way to treat a family. He was a great doctor, and although his face remained cold and his words were firm, he was honest, and it was obvious that he had dedicated himself to Josiah—and we respected him tremendously. But without remorse for being the only dry eye in the room, the doctor walked out and completed his rounds with the other children on the floor.

Jen held Josiah's tiny little body and began to cry. She curled her arms underneath Josiah and wrapped her hands around his body trying to embrace the final moments with her son.

"I love you so much," she whispered, holding him as tightly as the cords and tubes allowed. The tears fell from her cheeks, and she hugged Josiah with her last motherly instinct to protect him from the fate that waited. Nurse Kimmie stayed by Jen's side through the entire event.

That day we all cried over Josiah, but we all mourned for Jen.

Tears streamed down my face as I reached for Jen. I was never there for her when she was a child, and now her child would never be there either. Love had always been ripped away from her, and today, love would forever leave her side.

Just one more smile. Give us one more smile, Lord; one more laugh, I kept praying. It was what kept us going all those months in the hospital room. On Josiah's good days, we would play games and have tickle fights or give a cascade of kisses to bring the biggest smile to Josiah's face. Daisha would love to press her cheek next to Josiah's and hold his hand. She was still young and couldn't pronounce "brother" correctly, so each time she placed her head next to his, the phrase, "I love you, Bubby," became the closest sound to Heaven we ever heard.

Watching our grandkids laugh and smile together made our lives feel whole. From a life plagued by darkness, the days we could laugh and love together were always the brightest. It was our only refuge, and it was the only time where Josiah's climb seemed worth the fight.

It was why we needed one more smile from Josiah. It was why *I* needed one more smile from Josiah. I needed to see our family be happy together just one more time.

All morning I prayed and begged, but Josiah remained still.

God, he's with You now. He's with You.

* * *

Jen asked that the initial moment of Josiah being switched from the ventilator to the oxygen pump be a moment she experienced alone. Not that she didn't want us around, but in a sense, if Josiah was not going to make it off the ventilator, she only wanted her world to stop and not everyone else's.

The hospital called me with the instructions, and we proceeded to the hospital with Daisha in hand. For the next hour, Jen sat with the lights dimmed, listening to rain trickle down the windowpane, holding onto whatever moments she had left with her son.

Switching from a ventilator to an oxygen pump was part of Josiah's dying process. Josiah was barely holding on as it was, relying solely on a ventilator to breathe and morphine to keep his pain at bay. Any more of either and he would most likely remain a vegetable the rest of his life, but removing the ventilator could kill him before our family could return.

Before the rest of the medical team entered, Nurse Kimmie pushed open the door and took a seat with Jen. Since day one, the medical team was family, and Kim had been like a sister.

They shared the room of tears. Words continued to elude them, but the sound of the ventilator told the story they couldn't. Then finally, something struck Jen, and no matter how elusive words became, she used every bit of strength to look up at Kim and force out every sound through the wall of her emotions: "What will happen?"

Slightly confused, Kimmie looked at Jen, knowing something else was on her mind.

"What do you mean?"

"What will happen with his . . . body?"

"Well, I . . ."

"What I mean . . ." Jen drew a long but stagnant breath. "Can he be an organ donor?"

With tear-filled eyes, Kimmie said, "I'm really not sure because of the Progeria. I'm so sorry, Jen. I just don't know."

They both knew it. The fight was over.

*　*　*

We rushed back to the PICU, and the medical team entered the room and hugged us dearly. No words were said, but as they wrapped their arms around us, we felt everything they couldn't say. The thump of their hearts against our own, their clutched bodies wrapped around ours, and their eyes—teary and honest— told us they, too, were hurt and they, too, were fragile. We had never faced more pain in our lives, but in that hospital room, we had never felt more loved.

All of us huddled around Josiah's bed and looked at a child that was already gone. Colleen and Kimmie had been with us all day, and the reality of Josiah's situation finally hit them. We saw their eyes beginning to burn as Colleen turned away from the bed. Never once did we see them cry, but today, she turned to us and sobbed, "I'm sorry."

They were our rock and our leader, and the moment we saw them cry, our eyes began to swell, and I fell into the arms of my wife and Jen. It all became too real as our arms reached out for whatever was left of each other. In those moments, we became one. We felt the air slipping from Josiah's lungs, and experienced the emptiness when it escaped. We looked at each other but saw nothing at all. The tubes from his stomach reached from his rib cage to our own, and we no longer simply saw a coma—we were in one. Our world was caving in, and as Josiah was about to be taken out of his pain, a mother, a sister, a grandmother, and a grandfather were about to die.

The attending doctor eased his way toward Jen and me.

"A lot of people have been asking to see Josiah today. Would that be OK?" he asked.

Jen fought to maneuver words over the tears.

"Of course," she began. "But just as we discussed, we started this journey in Children's Two, and it's where I'd like it to end."

The doctor was a little taken aback by the request. The idea that our family was so loyal and thankful to the people in Children's Two surprised him. But he didn't see the sleepless nights the staff endured to distract Daisha while her little brother struggled through a four-hour surgery. He didn't feel the hands that comforted us when we couldn't hold ourselves up. He didn't hear the prayers whispered to a little boy as the staff bowed their heads beside us. The doctors, the nurses, and the staff on Children's Two were with Josiah every step of the way, and we owed them a real goodbye.

"We can arrange that," he ensured. "Just give us a moment."

A few minutes later another medical team entered the room and placed direct oxygen over his face. They were given strict orders to hold the pump directly over his mouth, because every time the pump angled off his face, his oxygen saturation levels would drop dramatically, starving his body of much-needed air. A nurse holding the oxygen steady hovered over Jen, and we traveled to Children's Two.

We exited the rattling double doors of the PICU, and my legs got heavy. The weight of Josiah's death all came rushing to me. I couldn't do it. The fact that we were walking to my grandson's death paralyzed me, and I stopped in the middle of the hallway. I looked down and saw the scuffs that we were now becoming and started crying to the Lord.

Words were never attainable, but we needed strength, and I needed God.

We got to the room as a crowd of people swarmed us. Doctors from each surgery and the medical staffs from each department all came to what seemed to be Josiah's living funeral. But the love radiating through each person made my heart reach for everyone there. The warmth and genuine affection for Josiah and love for this family drew me closer to God, and I found strength again knowing Josiah was in His hands. I guess it was just Josiah's time to go home, and I needed to make peace—maybe not at this moment, maybe not for a while—but I knew our only escape would be through peace.

The room was new to us but familiar all the same. We settled into yet another pleather seat and scuffed floor in a temporary foreign home. They kept this room like the PICU—dark, cold, and just dull enough to remind us of the numbing future we were about to enter.

But the time had come. The nurses put Josiah into his bed.

Please, one more smile, I begged to myself. *Just one more.*

But he lay there as lifeless as before.

The oxygen saturation levels were fading and the inevitable death couldn't have been much longer, but as our eyes were filling up with tears and his lungs were fading, his finger twitched.

I saw something. I most definitely saw something! I screamed in my head. I looked at Jen, and she saw it too. Some would say it was just the nerves still firing as his body was shutting down, but to my wife, Jen, and me, this was a sign—this was an invitation—and Josiah was trying to tell us something.

In the subtlest of voices, Josiah whispered, "Mommy."

This couldn't be happening, we all thought to ourselves. His voice was so faint that no one else in the room could hear, or believe, what we were telling them, but I knew this was not a mistake. This was a miracle.

I bent down and put my face in front of Josiah's. Knowing in my heart Josiah was there, knowing he was fighting, knowing he was meant to be with this family, I looked into his closed eyes and said, "Hi, Bubby."

And as if those words were his cue, Josiah's eyes shot open!

"He's awake!" Jen cried.

Josiah's arm sprung from the bed, and he grabbed my nose like he had done a thousand times. Then he looked into my eyes and gave the most wonderful smile we will never forget.

"My God. Get in here!" Jen yelled, "My baby's awake!"

11

HOME

JEN'S CRY ECHOED THROUGH Children's Two, and the medical staff rushed in. They couldn't believe it. Doctors rushed to inspect Josiah, and to everyone's surprise, he was awake and looking around the room like he had just woken up from a much-needed nap.

He was alive. With no plausible explanation, he was alive.

Tears of joy filled the room, but Josiah was far from out of the woods. As high as our spirits were for watching our little boy awake from a coma, Josiah's body was still just as critical as before. Like any loving grandmother, Deb had been saying since the first day he was sick, "Don't listen to the doctors! They only know what they see."

Her faith in our family finally resonated with everyone, but the reality remained that his body simply could not fight the infection and pneumonia, a collapsed lung, fluid in the other, all while fighting extreme malnourishment. So we tried to remain cautious for Jen's sake. To ask a mother to pull the plug on her own son then watch him wake up from a coma in her arms only to have him die minutes later would be a hell beyond anything imaginable.

But Josiah was alive.

And as much as we tried to remain calm and remain realistic—though the reality of my life now felt more like a fairytale—all I could do was hold onto the nurse's reminder: "God's not done with him yet."

* * *

After fifteen minutes and about a thousand kisses on Josiah's forehead, doctors reentered the room to do another checkup.

Still in shock from a survival no one believed to be possible, they evaluated him, their eyes still wide, as if they'd seen a ghost.

They checked his blood pressure, his heart rate, and then listened to his soft breathing. The young doctor slid his stethoscope around Josiah's chest as we watched and waited until we could hug our child again.

But the doctor gave a strange look to his colleague and checked Josiah's back. Then the front. Then the back. Something wasn't right.

Our minds instantly drifted to the worst, but I knew we were all reminded of the nurse's graceful words, *God's not done with him, God's not done with him.*

"Well," he paused trying to find the right words, but no words in the human language seemed to suffice. So, he said it plainly: "His lung is working."

Chills ran down my back.

We looked at each other in shock knowing this was no accident.

Doctors continued to inspect the functioning lung and called for a suction to once again drain the liquid from his right lung.

But we froze when they removed the suction tube and there was almost no fluid.

Within a few days his lung had healed.

With no medical assistance or any reasonable explanation, his lungs had completely and fully healed.

God's not done with him yet.

* * *

Josiah's health started to pick up steam, and we did our best to stay grounded (an impossible task at the moment). The medical staff continued to monitor Josiah's unexplainable progress and celebrated a victory no one saw coming. They had been upfront and honest with us the entire way, so when the word "miracle" was thrown around, we didn't take it lightly. And frankly, they just didn't know what would happen anymore.

As far as he'd come, his body still had a high possibility of giving out, and they warned us that he still quite possibility could die. But as the days passed, the medical books were thrown out the window.

Shocked but overjoyed more than ever before, Dr. Walsh left room 282 to return to the rest of her twenty-four-hour shift. She scribbled down the notes of what happened (seven pages' worth) to the attending medical staff with strict orders to page her immediately at any sign of decline. Josiah is a fighter, but his body was still on the brink of death, so she remained on guard for a page she thought would inevitably come.

Minutes passed.

Then hours.

No page.

She knew he was nowhere near stable, but she also knew this kid just would not stop fighting. Medically, it was just a matter of *when* his body couldn't sustain the fight anymore. It was coming, she knew it was coming, she was waiting for it to come, but after a few more hours passed, she checked her pager, and it stopped her in her tracks—no page.

"This kid's not gonna die," she whispered to herself. She knew Josiah would never give up, and it seemed like his body wouldn't either. Before she could process it, she looked out the window, and the sun began to rise.

* * *

My daughter held Josiah the entire night. Knowing at any minute a crash cart might rush into the room to try and revive Josiah's already depleted body, we sat on pins and needles waiting for something to happen. But as our anxiety and anticipation for the worst began to settle in for the night, the sun began to rise.

Drained and exhausted from her twenty-four-hour shift, Colleen came into the room to check on Josiah. He was alive. Again, as always, he was alive.

We laughed and then we cried; we hugged and then we talked. Emotions ran through Colleen like I had never seen, and she kept stressing that we needed to be very cautious in how we proceeded.

But he was still alive.

Though weakened and critically battered, we saw our little boy again. To everyone's surprise, he started to stabilize a little, but his infection was still life-threatening and could spike at any moment.

But he was still alive.

* * *

Then a second conversation emerged: going home. Hearing those words made the hair on the back of my neck stand at attention. Home? Only days before we were talking about pulling the plug on our little boy and now we were talking about home? It didn't seem real. It didn't seem possible. Then again, none of this did.

But the moment we let go of our own understanding and took a headfirst dive into faith, impossibility became irrelevant. This little boy was giving us every possible sign that he was more than a medical diagnosis—that he was more than a sad story, and that he was more than just another scuff on the hospital floor. God *is* most certainly not done.

As we prepared to take Josiah home, the floor once again filled with the same uneasiness we entered with. Josiah had regained function in his body and began to flourish, but his infection was not going away. Almost like this extra push of life was his temporary last stand, the medical team had an unspoken feeling they were only bringing Josiah to his house for the inevitable.

The medical staff gave us only a week's worth of medical supplies, never expecting Josiah to make it much longer. And it wasn't their fault. All reasonable statistics were leading to the same conclusion of an inevitable death. Everyone hoped for the best, but all common sense claimed he wouldn't even make the car ride home. The hospital was beyond treatment, and now was looking to keep him—and our family—as comfortable as possible.

* * *

"No one thought Josiah would ever make it out of the hospital; the fact he was going home—for however long that'd be—it was an astounding achievement." —Dr. Walsh

12

A MIRACLE

HOSPICE.

That's what they gave us.

Well, it was palliative care, but to us they were one and the same. Morphine to keep him "as comfortable as possible" while he inched toward a slow, bed-bound, deliberate crawl to death. There was no way we were letting our little boy fall victim to palliative care. We are, and always will be, his caregivers—palliative will not.

They told us he would never walk, never talk, and even if he was able to survive, he would be addicted to morphine the rest of his life. Alive or dead, they told us Josiah's life was over.

Colleen showed us how to check his feeding tube, how to change his abdominal dressing, how to feed him the nutrients he needed, and we began training. Years as an EMT helped, but you couldn't prepare for treating your own flesh and blood. We were wide-eyed students again, but Josiah deserved our best. Along with us in his corner, Colleen was there every step of the way. After each day practicing in his hospital bed, she told us a thousand times, "Just call me if anything happens. Just call."

Then, on October twenty-first, all of our practice was put to the test as we finally took Josiah home. We did everything Dr. Walsh trained us to do—changed the dressing over his now scar-tissued stomach each night, twisted the fifty cubic centimeter syringe to the tube from his nose and slowly pumped formula to his newly fixed intestine twice a day, and gave him round the clock service no 24/7 diner could match. But above all else, Jen walked into her little man's room and saw Josiah kicking and smiling every time she walked through the door. That was all she ever needed.

We knew his pain was through the roof. With a biogenetic mesh over his abdomen and an infection still burning through his intestines, morphine—so we thought—was the only option to keep him comfortable. Josiah seemed to us not to be in any pain. He acted like a normal child. As time went on, Josiah's local pediatrician, Dr. Gianfagna, came back into the picture. After the first or second visit to his office, he said to us, "I believe we can wean Josiah off the morphine." It was a shot in the dark. Without trying it, at best he would be a vegetable for the rest of his life. However, taking him off morphine could give him an excruciating death. But with all the other miracles we had witnessed, we had no trouble agreeing to give it a try.

Each day we gave him his standard medication and antibiotics, but we slowly started cutting down his morphine. Little by little, but Josiah didn't flinch. We prepared for the worst—withdrawal symptoms keeping him awake all night, crying all day, and squirming around his crib at all hours—but there was strength in this little boy that we had yet to discover. Not one symptom, not one tear. Finally, we stopped giving him morphine altogether.

Josiah didn't budge.

This was not hospice; this was his rebirth.

* * *

"Dad!" Jen frantically called from Josiah's room.

Oh no, I thought, *things are going so well, he couldn't have taken a turn for the worst.*

"Get in here! And bring a ruler . . ."

A ruler?

"A ruler?" I yelled upstairs, scrambling in search of the life-saving ruler I was expected to find.

"I'm serious! You need to see this!"

I grabbed an old wooden ruler I found in our kitchen drawer and ran up the stairs. Jen, hovering over Josiah with a starry-eyed glee I hadn't seen from my daughter since she was a schoolgirl, looked over at me and said, "Dad, it's shrinking." She started to giggle, "It's getting smaller."

I looked down at Josiah and saw exactly what she was trying to tell me. It was his stomach. As Jen was changing the dressing, she noticed that his flesh looked as if it were growing and making the opening around the mesh smaller. Due to all the scar tissue on his abdomen, we were told that his stomach would never grow over the genetic mess that was in place. I held the ruler over his stomach, eye-balling the diameter of the opening. The skin was starting to grow over the mesh. Now the ends looked like they were starting to reach for each other.

"It's definitely smaller," I said with a smile bubbling from my heart, and all I could see were Jen's eyes beginning to water. He was healing.

The world told us this would never happen.

The world told us palliative care was our only option.

The world told us to say goodbye.

But we saw something the world could not.

Over the next few weeks it continued to shrink. And a few weeks after that, it shrank some more. I kept thinking it in my head, but it was no longer a mantra—God was *truly* not done with this little boy, and there was one person that needed to know first.

"Colleen." She answered on the first ring and knew by my greeting we needed to get down to business.

"Hey, Dave. Is everything OK?"

"We have something to tell you."

"What's wrong? Is Josiah OK?"

"It's closed."

"What—" her voice dropped. "What do you mean it's closed?"

"His stomach. It healed over, Colleen."

She paused, and the few seconds of silence brought a smile to my face knowing our little man was going to be OK.

"Bring him in right way; we need to see him."

* * *

The next day we drove to Danville and once again entered Geisinger's Janet Weis Children's Hospital. We walked through the same halls, over the same treasure map carpet, and passed the same scratches on the floor, but this time was different. The dreary sight of walking down the hopelessly colorful hallways no longer was solitary confinement, but the final leg to a much-deserved home-run trot. The cold, scuffed hallways might as well have been a red carpet as Jen held Josiah like royalty all the way to the exam room. The dull plastic chairs no longer doubled as our living room furniture but a king's throne.

This was Josiah's triumph. This was his parade to the victory no one thought they would ever see.

Dr. Walsh walked in and hugged us closer than ever before. Tears came to her eyes, not in weakness, but in love. She held Josiah, and he latched onto her neck as if he knew about all the nights she spent at his bedside and felt the others she spent sobbing on her bedroom floor. She loves him with her entire heart, and she deserved this moment just as much as Jen did.

She examined Josiah's stomach, and to her shocking amazement, it had completely healed. She rubbed her hands up and down his torso to prove to her eyes that his wound was actually covered. Feeling his stomach and holding the boy she once lost, with a little smile, Dr. Walsh continued the exam. Temperature, blood pressure, heart rate: normal. No fever. No chills. No stuffy nose.

Dr. Walsh slid the stethoscope around Josiah's shoulders and heard nothing. No crackle, no hiss, and no blockage. She removed the stethoscope from her ears, and with a look of utter disbelief, she looked at us.

"He's—" she paused again and looked back at Josiah. "He's clean. One second."

She walked out of the room, and we saw her talking with the rest of the medical team. All at once they stormed toward the room and Dr. Walsh reentered, Dr. Scorpio following.

With a big smile on Dr. Walsh's face, she had Dr. Scorpio look at Josiah. Like usual, he sat down in his chair with his no-nonsense personality and a coarse demeanor that left no time for reintroductions. By this time, we had gotten to know Dr. Scorpio very well, and his straight-laced dedication to medicine was not taken harshly, but in comfort, knowing his attention to our little boy was second to none.

The room was thick with silence, and then Dr. Scorpio concluded the exam. But suddenly, hovering over Josiah, Dr. Scorpio
silently began to sob.

Through a hardened surgeon's teary eyes, Dr. Scorpio looked
at me, and I relived the moment Dr. Scorpio delivered Josiah's
death sentence. It seemed the diagnosis, the infection, the coma
were all street lamps guiding Josiah's life toward an inevitable
darkness and Dr. Scorpio had seen the destination a million
times before. But instead of the path we expected, Josiah was
given a torch, and he was told to lead. With each challenge, each
hurdle, each miracle, Josiah strengthened, and without any possible reasoning, Josiah survived.

Dr. Scorpio's tears fell to the floor and we were all at a loss.

Dr. Walsh looked at all of us, sharing red puffy eyes, wet from
sobbing, and with a big smile on her face, she said, "The infection
is gone. He's cleared."

The room fell silent.

No one gave an explanation, nor did they try. Josiah's victori-
ous fight for health hit everyone in the room harder than a death
sentence ever could, especially Dr. Scorpio. Now standing in the
doorway with tears in his eyes he said, "We did nothing to heal
this little boy. We did absolutely nothing."

PART 2

LIFE

In 2005, we were told to live through a story of a little boy's most certain death. We watched his story turn from confusion to certainty and couldn't find just one chapter that gave this little boy life. But as the coma set in, and Josiah's life was finally succumbing to his inevitable death, a new narrative began.

His coma ended the thread of a fate no one predicted. The Progeria diagnosis was still creeping into our minds, but now Josiah was given life, and we had to capture it before the diagnosis did. So we set off onto a new journey, and now we were faced with our greatest blessing and biggest challenge we never thought we would face: a childhood.

13

A CHILDHOOD | QUALITY OVER QUANTITY

JOSIAH WAS HEALTHY—RATHER, as healthy as he could be. For the first time in his life, Josiah was no longer bound to a hospital room but walking and talking like any young toddler—a feat every doctor claimed would never happen.

Our family tried to wrap our heads around Josiah's new life and understand why Josiah was spared. As we turned off the ventilator, I was not mistaken when I said we had to prepare for our lives to change forever, but no one could have ever imagined we would walk out of the hospital with Josiah alive. He was home, and to this day there still has not been one explanation for how Josiah survived. The word "miracle" is the only one that comes close to doing it justice. Progeria is still taking hold of his body, and nothing will change that, but death's clasp had been loosened, and Josiah was given a chance to be a kid.

Dr. Walsh told us that Josiah needed to experience life. He deserved to have friends, play sports, and have a real childhood. Sure, he was tiny and frail and maybe half the size of the other children his age, but after what he'd been through, there was nothing this side of the pale hospital walls that could hurt this little boy. Josiah was going to live his best life, and Dr. Walsh made sure of that.

No challenge was too great and no activity too dangerous. There was a way for Josiah to experience everything this world had to offer, and she made sure of it. He could now talk, he could now walk, and to Dr. Walsh, that meant Josiah was going to use all of his God-given abilities, no matter what.

* * *

Hutchinson-Guilford Progeria Syndrome gives a child about thirteen to eighteen years to live. Three of those years for Josiah had been spent in and out of hospitals. After what we went through in the hospital, I no longer worried about Josiah. He will live, he will grow, and he will flourish. God has made him to be something bigger than any of us could imagine, but I was scared to death for our family.

This family had been put through highs and lows that no one should endure, and Jen was given the worst of it. She was told to watch him grow up, to celebrate birthdays, to give him a childhood and give the rest of us a hope for the future, only to be told to say goodbye through Progeria's slow, cruel knife.

Josiah has been given to us for a reason, but no matter how great his purpose becomes, the ripping hole left in Jen's heart is a pain no one can fix, and it had slowly begun bleeding out. Josiah may have left the hospital and been told to live happily ever after—but she was not. As time went on, Jen began to change.

What were we supposed to do? Josiah was given a clean slate for only a couple more years, and now we were in charge of filling the page with every color under the sun before it was wiped away forever.

Jen and I began talking about his life and what was left of it.

We knew God gave us this child for a reason, but all we could see was more pain. What we went through was just the beginning of a journey we weren't sure we knew how to walk. It molded us, changed our relationships in ways we never planned, and finally, we broke.

The arguing, fighting, and the anger of my past that has haunted me since the nights I spent as a child curled up under my blanket crying began to flood my life once again. We built walls around each other, and the frayed ends of our lives began to unravel like never before.

The future became this dark horrid place that we wanted to run from. If only we could have crawled away from the world and hoped time missed us, then maybe we didn't need to think about outliving our child or didn't need to live within time's shadow, and then maybe, just maybe, we could be happy.

So we ran.

Just like I have done all my life, we hid from the reality we had to face. It was easy, and I was good at it. I ran from my childhood, ignoring it, pretending like nothing happened, and hoping it would just fade through time. I ran from my anger, the void that was in my heart spewing the words of a man that I despised, and like acid decaying a once-hardened enamel shell, the thought of our future only solidified the pain.

We didn't know what to do. I struggled with the thought of saying goodbye again, as did Jen, but we never spoke about it. We never counseled each other and never told each other how scared we truly were. I never told her about my sleepless nights wondering how we were supposed to love a child knowing he will only be ripped away or how we were supposed to love anything after he's gone.

And we never told each other that it was OK. It was OK to be scared and it was OK not to know our next step. And it was OK to mourn.

We didn't know how to say it. I didn't see the pain the love for her little boy gave to her, and I never thought that maybe accepting this new life was just as hard for her as it was for me.

We only needed each other, but even that we couldn't give.

We chose to hide from our problem and pretended we had no choice; that we could only live with anticipation of pain, leaving our lives as empty as the hospital room we came from. Our family started to splinter and rip at its seams, and slowly but surely, we lost sight of the gift of life God gave this little boy.

Jen and I tried to talk about our differences but mostly we focused on Josiah—it was all that we could do. The future still terrified us, but one night after the kids were asleep, our conversation broke. The idea of saying goodbye to Josiah so quickly after being given his miracle life cut to the core of our souls, but through a strength that was beginning to grow, Jen said, "Quality over quantity."

"What?" I replied, confused as to whether or not we were still on the topic of Josiah.

"For however long Josiah is with us." She stopped and fought back tears. "He's going to experience everything. He's going to live life. No matter what."

I looked at her, realizing what this meant. We were accepting the fact that Josiah's miracle would be through his life, and by his death we would absorb every ounce of pain that was left in his wake. Until this point, we had fought tooth and nail with death and we never gave in.

But avoiding death did not give us life.

It separated us, frightened us, and pushed us further away from the love that we fought so hard to find, and tonight we finally chose life by embracing death rather than fearing its arrival.

"OK," I said to her, understanding our line between life and death would forever be blurred. "Let's give him everything we can."

It wasn't the first time we talked about death, but it was the first time we didn't fight it. Death was coming, and we were going to face it together. Like every step of this journey, my faith was tested again and again. I still don't know how we are going to handle the reality of potentially watching our little boy be lowered into the ground, but we made a vow to give him everything we could for the time he is above it. That's what we can do for him now; and it's the only thing that matters.

Sometimes we pray, asking God for miracles in our lives, asking God for the food we need, asking God for anything and everything, but we forget that God knows what we need before we even ask. The fact that Josiah survived and is now living a life no one had any reason to believe in is not a testament to our faith; it's a testament to God's sovereignty.

We fall when we try to make God a genie in a bottle, granting wishes and prayers because good Christians were faithful. In the Book of Acts, the same day Peter was freed from prison, James was killed. They were both God's prophets, both believers in Christ, and both worthy of being saved. But it is not up to our faith to determine our time on earth; it is for God and God alone.

* * *

We had to forfeit his adulthood to regain his childhood. We knew his window was small—and closing by the second—but our lives could not, and will not, be lived looking to the future or fixating on the past. We only have this instant. And good or bad, we were going to capture it.

It was our first step toward life, but in order to move forward, Jen and I had to let go of our pasts. It was just too much. We had failed for years trying to carry our pasts individually, and we finally realized we could not find peace in spite of each other. We could only survive as a family, and we had to rely on one another.

As confused and haunted as we were, we searched for clarity, and searched for God. I guess you can say my faith welled up inside me. I can't speak for my daughter, but I felt a deep purpose for why Josiah was born to our family with such a rare disease. I started to find comfort knowing God gives special children to special people, and our family was no exception. God knew what was in store for Josiah, and all I could do was trust Him.

So through good and bad, we began to accept who we were and who we couldn't be.

As my wife's medical problems built, Jen took care of her, and I took care of the kids. We worked together to keep our family united, and slowly our lives began to come back. Jen and I started to find common ground, and our family grew stronger.

Things were never perfect, but we didn't need them to be. We stopped searching for perfection and started accepting everything we couldn't change. Jen and I dove back into our working agreement that turned into the start of a relationship. Sometimes we'd get mad, argue, or even feel like our lives together would never work, but through our weakest hour we tried to let go; and more importantly, we tried to love.

Josiah was given a life, and now we were going to let him experience it. Through the good and bad we started to function like a family, and in the process, we found the beginning of a restoring love that gave us a life—our life.

Quality over quantity.

14

MIRACLE CHILD

I N 2007, WE WERE back at Janet Weis Children's Hospital for a routine checkup and couldn't be happier to see Dr. Walsh. Jen and I continued to journey on the unfamiliar road of sincerity, and we started working together as a family like we did in room 282. But today, we re-entered these halls like royalty, and with every turn, we heard the whispers, "That's him, that's the miracle child," as if the hospital had just seen a character from a fairytale.

We walked into the exam room, and Dr. Walsh—now Josiah's pediatrician—was so excited to greet us, her eyes filled up with tears. She hugged Josiah and then hugged us all. Everyone in the hospital knew how much Dr. Walsh cared about Josiah and how much we trusted her. From the frantic three a.m. phone calls to the times we expected Josiah to die, Dr. Walsh fought for us and fought for Josiah's life. Her work didn't go unnoticed, and her superiors knew how special this little boy was to her, so they made Josiah her outpatient; her very first one, and to this day, Daisha and Josiah are still her only two.

She continued to examine Josiah, and I looked through the door to see Jen laughing and chatting with someone in the hallway. In the middle of their talk, Jen waved for me to meet this person. I figured it was a family friend I couldn't recognize or just another person who had heard the tale of Josiah Viera—in the past year his story had spread through the hospital like wildfire, so I wouldn't have been surprised if it were yet another person trying to see this "Miracle Kid," as the hospital floor dubbed him. So I walked over, and Jen introduced me.

Her name was Bonnie Tharp. She was a kind, middle-aged woman from the Children's Miracle Network and lived close to our hometown, so when Josiah's story traveled through the medical world, she was one of the first to investigate. Bonnie had been with CMN for almost five years and was—and is—very passionate about the work she does—the archetype of who should be involved in the charitable organization.

Jen explained Josiah's condition and all the confusion that had led to his coma. They talked about Children's Two, the surgeries, all the moments we thought it was the end, and they talked about the future and whatever that could mean.

She told us the story of a Josiah Viera had been circulating the Children's Two, a CMN network hospital, and she just had to meet the family. She was sincere, and a genuinely loving person, and I couldn't help but be impressed. Jen looked at me and then looked at Bonnie. "Would you like to meet him?"

Like most people, she lit up over the idea of meeting this little boy whose story had become more of a folktale than medical actuality.

"I would be honored," she replied with a smile.

* * *

"How can someone meet Josiah and not fall in love?" she said after exiting the room. She looked ready to cry. "I just cannot get over that little boy's smile."

At this point Josiah still had hair—Progeria kids are born with hair and quickly lose it to their aging process—and still had very rough, thin skin. We knew his look captured people, but what I didn't realize was his face. The whole time we were meeting with Bonnie, he laughed and smiled. We brought him to the hospital, he smiled. We went back home, he smiled. His smile is so much a part of who Josiah is, we didn't even realize its novelty until other people told us how grabbing it truly is. But that's who he was, and that's who he is today. This theme continued, and we began to notice he was an overwhelmingly happy little boy.

Even today, Josiah is always smiling. And it was not a forced, taught laugh; this was innate. Something inside this little boy had been tuned and inherently given a chord of happiness, and we just didn't know why.

We began working with Bonnie and the Children's Miracle Network ever since Josiah left the hospital. It was mostly small gatherings—meeting people or simply telling Josiah's story. Josiah's story continued to spread so quickly it became an out-landish story you assumed was just a fable, so people wanted to hear it from the source. We'd go to Geisinger events, and al-most everyone gathered around to meet the child behind all the tales they'd heard. Everyone was real nice, and they couldn't get enough of Josiah.

He loved it.

Josiah loved being the center of attention and enjoyed the spotlight. But through all the hugs and commotion of the room, his smile continued to amaze. After every event, every medical practitioner, CMN workers, and even news reporters kept rav-ing about how wonderful this little boy's smile was. People were dazzled by it. They saw the happiness inside this little boy and wanted it for themselves. How could a little boy so damaged, so sick radiate with such a glow? It became the question everyone asked us, and a question they started to ask themselves.

* * *

This now folktale, heroic story was nominated for one of the Children's Miracle Network "Miracle Children" of the Wilks-Barre/ Scranton area. Once a patient's story is submitted, it is reviewed by the CMN selection committee, and about two-to-four stories for each region of the state are chosen for a final review. The infec-tion, the coma, the healing, and the rare case of Progeria jumped off the page, and at age three, Josiah was instantly selected.

Being a regional Miracle Child is a unique honor. It's designed to give the child the sense of recognition and achievement for bat-tling a life-threatening disease but brings quite an undertone of sadness knowing the circumstance that the children are facing. It gives the patient and their family certain experiences that may never have happened, while celebrating the life and the fight of each tough kid.

The children and their families get to have once in a lifetime experiences, and CMN gives sponsors another reason to donate.

Once Josiah was a Miracle Child, Walmart, the major CMN sponsor, invited us all to their local store to meet the corporate staff.

Once the small introduction was over, they told Jen to fill a basket with whatever she wanted. Food, clothes, supplies, anything the family might need, throw it in the cart. They finished shopping, and the sponsor presented our family with a Visa gift card loaded with $1000. It was a great event for both CMN and us, but before we left, the sponsor took Josiah over to the toddler section and told him to pick out a toy. You should have seen the look on Josiah's face. He stopped and told the director in the strongest voice he could that he didn't want anything here. The sponsor was confused and asked Josiah why not. Josiah looked up and said, "'Cause these are baby toys."

The sponsor realized he mistakenly transposed Josiah's size for his age and felt terrible for his assumption. He knew Josiah was turning four soon but figured he still played with toys more his size. He quickly apologized, but it was a common mistake. Josiah was barely two feet tall and was just starting to gain weight, so everyone treated him as he looked—like a baby.

Then he picked Josiah up and quickly walked over to the "big boy" section and told him, "Pick out anything. Anything you want. As much as you want."

* * *

Josiah's story deserved to be told and his life deserved to be celebrated, but we were a bit scared of everything that was happening. The media, the exposure, and all the people wanting to meet our little boy became overwhelming. We wanted to give Josiah everything but didn't want him to feel pressured or become propaganda for some moneymaking machine—even if it is a nonprofit. He wasn't a prop or a face for donations, he was a kid, and we wanted to make sure it stayed that way.

So, we decided to take it slow. We would go to an event and see how Josiah liked it. If it became too taxing on him, or just didn't feel right, we would leave. Simple as that. But we quickly discovered Josiah loved it. He loved meeting new people and loved the events the Children's Miracle Network set up. Maybe it was the ice cream, the pictures with Santa, or just Josiah being a ham for the camera, but he was enjoying every minute of the events and our worries slowly faded.

If he was happy, so were we.

Quality over quantity.

Over the next year, we were introduced to some of our local celebrities and had the opportunity to be on television. We met our region's most popular radio personality, Drew Kelly from WQKX, and then had a full documentary on our local television station. We may have just been wide-eyed country folk from the central PA mountains, but Josiah was a movie star! The phone was ringing off the hook from our family and friends back in Hegins after the programs aired. Josiah was famous! We were on local radio and television! When Bonnie told us they wanted us to be on the CMN telethon on television, I think our jaws hit the floor.

We were nervous, but through a big smile and a giggling little voice, we realized Josiah was excited. He loved talking with people and being in the spotlight, and now he was getting a chance to do so with a great organization. They interviewed us at our house and put together a very nice story, but we were nervous about going live.

Live television!

We got on set and saw all the phones, met the hosts, and got ready for our segment. And it went off without a hitch. They interviewed us about Josiah's journey and played the documentary. I still remember the moment the red light flashed on top of the camera and a man with a headset pointed to our host, Eric Deabill. As he lifted his microphone, Josiah was no longer a local celebrity; he was about to become a national wonder. That night was so much fun, but little did we know that local television was only the beginning and what God had in store would change our lives forever.

Each year after that, the CMN would beg Josiah to come to the telethon. After the influx of donations, it made sense to have him on camera as much as possible. We realized people wanted to hear Josiah's story and it boosted sponsorship. But CMN treated our family like royalty, and Josiah loved the attention, so why not? Today Josiah usually doesn't want to go on donor trips or sponsorship gatherings, so we simply don't go. But it was Josiah's first taste of being somewhat of a celebrity, and it was our first glimpse of how people would react to his journey.

* * *

In 2008, Bonnie told us Josiah was nominated to represent Pennsylvania as a National Miracle Child. We laughed it off because we thought there was no way little Josiah Viera from Hegins, Pennsylvania, would ever be chosen. There are thousands of applicants, and the final decision comes down to the national headquarters in Utah. It was a far-fetched idea, so we told her we truly appreciate her nominating us, but we didn't expect much to come from it.

Every time I thought it couldn't possibly get better, God would show me I am not the one in control. He is.

A couple of weeks later, we got a phone call from Bonnie.

"Hello," Jen answered.

"Josiah's been picked," she said without even saying hello. "You guys are representing Pennsylvania as a National Miracle Child! You're going to Walt Disney World!"

We really didn't know what to say. Not that we didn't believe Josiah should have been picked, but we couldn't comprehend how far this story traveled in such a short amount of time. It felt like we were just shot out of a cannon. Josiah, the Pennsylvanian representative, was one of about fifty-five kids in North America going to Disney to represent their states at a national convention. It was unreal. Jen shared the news, and we jumped and shouted. We began laughing, and half-jokingly I said to her, "Things can't get any greater than this. They just can't get any better, right?" She cut me off before I could go any further and said, "Dad, stop saying that! Every time you say that, it gets better."

15

YOU'RE GOING TO DISNEY WORLD

JOSIAH SKIPPED THROUGH HARRISBURG International Airport in his t-shirt and ball cap, ready to battle the Florida sun, and we were stuck pulling the luggage and looking for our plane. I started to think there was a reason for all of this. I knew the travel, the interviews, and even the notoriety had become taxing on us, but this was no accident, and we were starting to see threads of His master plan being sewed together. We still didn't fully understand why or how this was happening, but we weren't meant to connect the dots just yet. Right now, we were supposed to enjoy a vacation as a family and see our little boy experience life to the fullest; and right now that was all that mattered.

We got to the hotel and were welcomed by a party of guests. Mickey and Minnie Mouse, Donald Duck, Disney Princesses, and all the sponsors for the Children's Miracle Network were waiting and cheering at our arrival. The kids loved it. They watched movies and had a few snacks on the flight down as new friends, so this was a celebration they enjoyed together.

The convention is the Children's Miracle Network's biggest event of the year and invites their biggest donors and sponsors for an all-inclusive stay at Disney World. They gave us our room keys and check-in gifts for the kids, and we were set for five days and five nights in a Disney suite.

The ballroom looked like the size of a football field. Decorated as if we were about to have tea with the queen, the white tablecloths matched the cotton gloves worn by every busboy hustling around the room making sure everything was spotless. They reconstructed the room to have three rows of tables, one for each Miracle Child, to make a steady flow of people walking up and down an aisle for each sponsor to meet the children and get their programs autographed. Like many kids there, Josiah couldn't write, so Jen wrote his name on a piece of paper, and the planning crew made a stamp Josiah could push onto every program.

The meet and greet was about to start, and each Miracle Child took a seat at their own table. The doors opened, and hundreds of people started filtering through the aisles, and the place was packed. It was a fun chance to meet everyone and give the kids a sense of stardom. They were the celebrities, and the convention really made them feel like it was a red-carpet event. Josiah was stamping everyone's program, taking pictures, and loving every minute of it. Jen, Bonnie, and I sat with him at the table but stayed in the background. This was his time, and we were just there to soak it all in. But before I knew it, I picked my head up, and a line had formed, stretching out the entrance door. I figured it was the line to get in, but as I looked around, I saw the line went directly to Josiah's table, cutting across the entire room.

The line grew, and almost every person in the ballroom was waiting for Josiah. Jen, Bonnie, and I looked at each other and realized this was getting a little out of control. People were intentionally skipping the previous two aisles to meet Josiah. Bonnie looked at me a bit worried and said, "I feel kinda bad. They're only trying to see Josiah."

I scanned the other tables and saw rows of kids just sitting there, waiting, with no one at their tables. We began to feel terrible, but what could we do? The line of people started to congregate around Josiah, and the other tables emptied. I stepped out from behind the table and yelled to the back of the line, "There are other kids other down here!" while pointing to the obvious tables they had bypassed to get to Josiah.

The group looked around realizing the unfair crowd that had formed.

"Maybe they can give you an autograph first!" I yelled, trying not to sound rude.

A few people left after realizing there were still over a hundred people in line before them; so they got a few autographs then circled back to the line. The longer we were down there, the more people became intrigued by who this little boy was. It was unbelievable.

Josiah was still tiny and was starting to develop the natural look of a Progeria child—skinny legs, bulging knees, thin, wrinkly skin—but there were a lot of other kids battling something way more destructive than he was. One little boy had no legs and no arms and was a joyful, happy seven-year-old. He was a true inspiration and a brave soul. Every child there was fighting something visibly terrible, but everyone was glued to Josiah. It wasn't his look, it wasn't his size; there was something more people were attracted to, and right then I knew this trip would be more than a vacation.

But our vacation would have to wait because Josiah was exhausted and ready for bed.

We started back to our room and I tried to digest everything that had happened. We never expected how quickly people would gravitate toward Josiah or the explosion of attention he would draw. It was overwhelming, to say the least, but he handled it like a pro. He was poised and confident. Barely five years old, Josiah looked like a seasoned celebrity delighted by a group of fans. A normal five-year-old is not expected to handle something like that so elegantly, but maybe he wasn't just a normal five-year-old.

*　　*　　*

The trip continued to unfold just the way it started. People couldn't get enough of Josiah, and his story rattled through the convention like it was the only story being told. For the next few days, we had a full camera crew following us around for yet another CMN documentary and even did a commercial with big CMN donor, Rob Schneider. All the children's stories were incredible in their own right and deserved to be heard, so the convention made sure that every child was given some spotlight. But people became personally attached to Josiah. The crowds began to overwhelmingly sail well beyond the standard spotlight and became something bigger than we could ever imagine.

At the time, I was a huge fan of Glenn Beck and I found out he was one of the speakers at the convention. He is one of CMN's biggest donors and gives a talk each year to all the corporate sponsors. But we weren't invited to this one. You had to pay, and you needed a suit. It was a black-tie event. I never even owned an expensive suit; I just couldn't afford it. And quite honestly, if it wasn't for the Children's Miracle Network paying our expenses to get down here and Walmart's donation of a $1,000 gift card to our family, our trip would have never had happened. We never had much money, so extra things like this had always been out of our reach.

But I found out he was speaking at the same ballroom we had the meet-and-greet in a few days before and decided to try and see him. I pulled out the nicest clothes I owned: a blue collared shirt from last year and my only pair of khaki pants. Well, they were my khaki shorts, but it was my only decent outfit, and I thought I looked nice.

I walked down to the convention hall and tried to sneak in the side door. Locked. I tried the other one. Locked. I looked for another door to slide through but quickly realized my 007-mission would have to be completed through the main entrance. Just blend in, shake his hand, and leave. The event had already started, and people were filling their seats. As I inched closer to the entrance, I realized there was no way I could get in. Security was everywhere, and I was not going to look like a fool on my grandson's vacation.

So I stood out in the hallway with the cleaning ladies and watched. The speech had to extend well over an hour until people finally started filing out the door. Tuxedos and gowns I had only seen at weddings whizzed by as the people wearing them looked past me. I guess since I wasn't dressed in a three thousand-dollar tux these people didn't feel the need to acknowledge my existence. Platinum watches and diamond necklaces filled the hallways, and I pushed through to try to catch a glimpse of Glenn. As I looked around, I saw him walk backstage—he was gone.

I walked back to the family a little disappointed, but I tried to shake it off, as this vacation was not about me. But like a kid who just missed seeing his idol, I kept bringing up his tie and telling the family what he looked like.

"He's gotta be six feet, no probably six foot one. I mean he was a big guy and his tie?! Ha. I wouldn't expect anything less," I rambled on to the response of eye rolls and lip service to get me to stop talking about it.

The next day I carried on about my missed opportunity, and to put salt on my wounds, one of the sponsors from Walmart heard my continual pouting and said, "You wanted to meet Glenn Beck?"

"Yeah," I said hesitantly, figuring this was not the time or place for a political debate.

"Well, why didn't you say something? We had a backstage gathering with him and would have taken you along!"

"HA!" I blurted out half sarcastic, half deflated. "You've got to be kidding me."

Once the sting passed, I couldn't help but smile at the thought of how easy it could have been to meet him. We all got a good laugh and Jen said, "Hey, he's probably at the park today, you never know!"

"Yeah right. There's like ten parks here and about a million people. I missed my only chance."

We entered Disney's Narnia display building and I looked outside. Jen started violently waving her arm, pointing to my right, and obnoxiously looked at me with her eyes wide open and said, "Oh yeah, you aren't gonna see him? Oh yeah?"

I quickly ran to the entrance to get a glimpse of Glenn, but by the time I arrived, he disappeared with his family into a nearby building.

My own grandson woke up from a coma and yet I still thought Glenn Beck was an unreachable star? I guess God does have a sense of humor and wanted to prove to me that I was not done growing.

As we left the Narnia building we walked only a few feet before Jen leaned over the stroller and sarcastically sang, "Ohh Da-ad," then pointed over my shoulder. I quickly turned. To everyone's surprise, it was Glenn Beck walking right toward us with his son on his shoulders, his wife on his right, and his bodyguard to his left.

And here he came.

No paths to jump, no crowds to weave through; Glenn Beck was not only walking on the same route as us, but he was also headed directly for us.

"Mr. Beck?" Jen asked as confidently as she could.

"Yes," he said with a slight hesitation as if wondering who was asking.

"I'm Jennifer Viera and this is my family. We're big fans of yours. This is my son, Josiah Viera,"

"Josiah?!" he shouted in astonishment.

I froze. How did he know that? How did Glenn Beck know Josiah's name?

"Yes, this is my grandson, Josiah Viera, and this is his mother, Jennifer Viera."

"Well it's a pleasure to meet you," he said with a big smile. Then he bent down to shake Josiah's hand. "Josiah! How're you doing, man?"

He talked with us for a few minutes, and as it turns out, the CMN chose a few stories from the convention to play at the sponsors' seminar, and Josiah's was played for all to see.

I was starstruck when he said he saw Josiah's story at the same convention room I couldn't get near. For a brief moment I pondered whether there were any dry eyes in the room that day. He didn't say, and I didn't ask.

I had to pause and laugh. This was comical, but Glenn had no idea. I didn't have the heart to tell him that as every millionaire sat in a chair I couldn't afford, wearing clothes I couldn't buy, watched the story of our little boy, my collared shirt and khaki shorts couldn't even get through the doors.

It was incredible to finally meet him, but we didn't want to hold him up any longer than we already did. We thanked him for being part of the Children's Miracle Network, shook his hand, and parted ways. We began walking again, and I was hovering on cloud nine. Pushing the stroller alongside me, Jen nudged my arm and gave me the biggest sarcastic smile: "See?" And even though she was only kidding, she was right.

This trip to Florida couldn't have been scripted any better, and it was time I finally let God take over. We always try to control what's happening or try to figure out the next step. But our finite minds will not ever be able to conceive the magnitude of God's will, and it was time I stopped trying.

Yes, meeting Glenn Beck was incredible and some could call it lucky. But knowing Glenn Beck saw our little man's story a few days before we happened to run into each other in an amusement park full of a few hundred thousand people is not lucky—it's intentional. And it was time we started to enjoy the ride God had in store for Josiah and the gift he had in store for us.

16

JOSIAH'S GIFT

AFTER A VACATION FILLED with Disney characters and ice cream sundaes, the convention was coming to a close. The last day at Disney was the medal ceremony for all the Miracle Children. Each year, the CMN rolls out the red carpet to give each child their official medal for being selected as one of the year's "Champions." It was the grand finale of the convention and truly a rock star event.

We entered the same gigantic ballroom as the meet-and-greet, but this time the room was lined with chairs facing an extravagant stage stretching the width of the room. Neon floodlights lit the ballroom while thick spotlights directed our attention to the glass-like floors and illuminated staircase wrapping around the front of the stage. Cameras swiveled around the room and music played while we all found our seats. It looked like a movie set at one of the Disney parks we had just returned from, and the show was finally about to begin.

Hundreds of people filtered into the seats, and touring artist and Academy of Country Music award-winner Mark Wills walked on stage along with that year's Miss America pageant winner to host the event. After an evening of laughs, music, and a few heartwarming videos of the convention highlights, it was time for the Miracle Children to receive their awards.

Josiah was already backstage standing in line with rest of the kids waiting for their names to be called, and we sat on the edge of our seats waiting to see Josiah's time in the spotlight. They announced each child individually to walk, if able, or to be pushed across the stage to be presented with their champion medal. As children began to cross, a steady stream of applause followed. A few cheers or sharp whistles from the crowd easily identified each champion's family, but the applause remained tame as an uplifting instrumental played in the background. It was very nice and allowed each child to have their time on the big stage.

And then a little boy came to the corner of the stage.

Mark Wills lifted his microphone and said, "Representing Pennsylvania, Josiah Viera!" And the place erupted.

Barely twenty-four inches tall, he stepped forward through thunderous applause in his toddler khaki pants hanging over his Velcro-fastened shoes, with his child's small t-shirt draped around his shoulders.

By the time Mark Wills finished announcing Josiah's name, everyone was on their feet. The levels drowned any other sound in the room and Josiah bounced across stage with the biggest smile on his face. The applause became deafening, and I began to cry as it all made sense to me.

I realized these people weren't just clapping because he's cute or tiny. They were cheering because they saw something more than a child with a disease; they saw more than a survivor or inspiration—they saw hope. They saw a little boy with an infectious, God-given personality they couldn't explain. They saw a joyful spirit they knew was beyond the grasp of a disease. They saw his journey turn into a miracle, and in some way, knew they could complete their own.

Unless someone experiences it themselves, no one will ever be able to truly understand what it's like to wake up from a coma and then heal from a deadly infection only to be greeted with a terminal disease. But they don't have to understand it, because Josiah lives it. He proves that joy will always overcome pain, and God's light can be found through any storm.

So they took what they needed: happiness, joy, the will to fight, the strength to overcome, the courage to find acceptance, the heart to forgive, and they became the recipients of something more than just a medal. So they cheered and cheered and found what they never knew they had been searching for.

Because sometimes, the only way God can send His message is through a little boy dancing across a stage.

Josiah hustled toward Mark Wills, swimming in his big t-shirt with an even bigger smile stretched across his face, and it was all finally clear. Right there, we knew this moment was the reason he was on this earth, and this reaction was why his impact will forever remain.

My wife and I shared a tissue. We wiped our eyes and looked at Jen with smiles on our faces. We talked about our journey and remembered all the times this family had quit, gave up on each other, divided and rejected one another, and now we both saw that God gave this special little boy to our family because we needed him more than anyone else.

What our family didn't know was the years spent in the hospital had meticulously blended our lives together. Before any of this, the only thing we shared was a silent pain. We suffered alone and slowly killed ourselves by bottling the pain within ourselves. It was our own pain, our own lives, and we broke apart because we lost the only aspect of life that keeps us living—love.

Now, we were no longer introduced to sorrow alone, but rather as a family. The scars worn on our hearts were still there, but they became a reminder of what we've been through. My buried past of an abusive childhood and our ugly struggle with self-acceptance became the Hell that led us toward Heaven.

In those moments, we saw what we had been searching for the entire time: forgiveness. We had to forgive one another, but also ourselves. For years, we tried to heal alone, to clean up our own lives and then maybe our family's life could follow. But healing is sometimes shared, and it comes from understanding that God requires us to forgive one another as He forgives us. As we accepted our imperfections and leaned on one another during Josiah's years in the hospital, our broken individual pieces came together, and we started the journey to become whole.

The Lord forever works in mysterious ways, and what was once a battle we couldn't win, with the Lord and each other, had become a battle we couldn't lose. Our separated future became a journey walked together. We had started to become a family, and in that ballroom in Florida, we had started to become a home.

The place was still on their feet, and Josiah's medal was hung around his neck. As he crossed the stage, we looked around and finally knew without a doubt, this was real.

We gave our last cheer, then with tears in our eyes and joy in our hearts, my wife and I crossed the floor to meet Jen and Josiah and I began to joke, "OK, it can't get any bett—"

"Dad," she cut me off with a grin. "Don't even say it."

17

AN INTRODUCTION TO THE GAME OF BASEBALL

IN THE SPRING OF 2009, Josiah was about to turn five years old. He stood only twenty-three inches tall and weighed less than twenty pounds. Almost every night, Daisha and the neighborhood boys would be in the yard playing baseball. Like any other little boy standing off in the distance watching, Josiah wanted to join the game.

From the moment we got home they would be outside playing baseball until it got dark, and Josiah would watch from the back porch like a devout fan unable to get through the gates of Yankee Stadium. One day, Josiah walked over and joined in. I'm not sure if they asked him, or if he just decided he would take part, but when I looked outside, Josiah was swinging a plastic bat twice his size while a tennis ball came hurtling toward him.

He was so little compared to the other kids; I didn't want him to get hurt, so I rushed outside. I explained to the boys they needed to be extra careful around Josiah, and before I could say anything more, Josiah spoke up.

"Pap, I want to play baseball with my friends," he told me, pleading his case in his high-pitched voice.

I admit, I was a little nervous, but we decided it was OK to play baseball. I told them just be careful—please, be very careful. The boys assured us they would take care of him and told us not to worry. Although the reassurance from a nine-year-old kid firing a tennis ball around the yard was not as comforting as I'd hoped, I guess they did have a point. They were just having fun playing stickball, so who was I to take that away?

They played for weeks. Rain or shine, they were outside playing ball until dark. Jen, Nana, and I would watch from the back porch, but Daisha and the boys took care of Josiah.

He looked forward to playing ball every chance he got. Sometimes, we had to go get him and bring him in the house because it was dark out, but he would have played all night if he had the chance.

Then one day we heard a knock at the door. I peeked through the windows and saw the neighborhood boys standing on our back porch. As I opened the door, I called Josiah to tell him his friends were here.

"Wait," one of the boys started. "We want to . . . umm . . . talk to you," he stumbled through. "I, we, promise to ask our dad first but we wanted to ask . . . Can Josiah play on our Little League team?"

By this time, Jen heard the conversation, and it caught me so off guard that I didn't know how to respond—but I didn't need to.

"I want to play! I want to play!" Josiah yelled.

Knowing Josiah's love of playing baseball in the backyard, we couldn't say no. But we knew it was going to be a hard sell to the leadership of the local Little League.

"I'm gonna play Little League!" Josiah shouted after we agreed, but we told him it was not up to us, and we didn't want him to be disappointed if they said no. Josiah would have none of it. He was certain he was going to play Little League.

The boys thanked us and went running back to their house. The next day we talked to Sam, the head coach of the Tri-Valley White Sox and president of the town's Little League. Sam and his wife sat in our living room. Like most folks from the mountains here in the tri-valley, they were very polite and kind, hardworking, generous to others, and humble—our kind of people.

We talked about the logistics of Josiah playing Little League. Like everyone else, they were concerned about safety, and we were, too. Not just for his personal well-being, but liability as well. We understood their concern, but I knew Josiah would be crushed if he couldn't play. I turned to Sam and said, "Look, we get it. It's nerve-wracking for us, too, but it's just one game. Let him hit once and run to first. And that will be it." We told them we would sign any waiver they needed; we just wanted Josiah to have fun.

After a little back and forth, they agreed. By this time, it was dark out, and the kids were back from their pick-up game. Sam turned to Josiah and bent down next to him and said, "Well, looks like were gonna let you play baseball with the big boys!" The kids started to laugh and give each other high fives, as if this was their secret plan all along.

* * *

We ordered the smallest size available, children's extra small. It was just a black, cotton t-shirt with "Tri-Valley White Sox" printed on the front and "Josiah Viera" on the back, but it was his first baseball uniform, and he couldn't have been more excited.

We pulled it over his head, and it looked more like an apron hanging from his neck with his shoulder popping out from the collar, but Josiah didn't care. It was *his* jersey, and this was *his* new team.

A pair of white baseball pants and his favorite pair of sneakers topped off his uniform. The team gave him the smallest baseball hat they could find, but as much as he bent the peak trying to maneuver this bucket into a wearable accessory, it was no use and kept falling down his face. A few more adjustments made the hat balance around his ears—close enough. He was now a Tri-Valley White Sox and ready for his first baseball game.

I put our pickup in park outside the Little League complex while a dozen black baseball hats ran on the outfield grass. Sam walked up and down the foul line trying to make some order of the nine-year-old chaos, and I looked back to Josiah in the car seat. I could tell he was excited. Watching him quietly stare through the car window at the other boys I said, "Hey, Bubby, just have some fun today, OK?" He nodded his head with a big smile on his face and said, "OK, Pappy!"

The game started, and we watch the Tri-Valley White Sox take on the parental rival from the neighboring town. Well, maybe they weren't actual rivals, because the way the parents cheered and yelled for their kids, you would have assumed we were playing their next of kin.

As each inning came to a close, my stomach churned a little as Josiah's at bat approached. I don't know if I was nervous or excited. Maybe both.

3rd inning: *It's just one at-bat. He'll hit the ball and touch first. He will be fine.*

4th inning: *Just hit the ball and touch first. Just touch first. Touch first. He'll be OK—he will be OK—it looks like he's having fun.*

5th inning: *OK, he's having a blast!*

The 6th inning ended, and both teams began cheering as the PA announcer called Josiah to the plate. The players helped slide a team helmet over his new hat, and Josiah walked to home plate with Sam. He put the bat on his shoulder and Sam adjusted his feet. But as Josiah got to the plate, any anxiety I may have had faded away.

Josiah was in his element, and it was our job to let him have fun.

Sam grabbed a few baseballs and took a knee on the dirt in front of the mound. Josiah tapped the plate twice and reached back, ready to hit.

Sam flipped the first baseball toward Jo, and *ping*! He hit it! Josiah put all he could into his swing but could barely take the bat fully around his body. *He hit the ball!* It didn't go far—maybe five, six feet—but Josiah saw it hit the ground and took off running. We put our hands up and gave a loud cheer for our little man: "Go, Bubby!"

His pants were falling down, jersey was flapping everywhere, helmet was bouncing down over his eyes, and he was going as fast as his little legs could move.

With his teammates cheering him down the line, Josiah made it to first with a big leap, landing on top of the base with both feet. He looked over to his coach, and with a thumbs-up sign let out a big yell: "Yeah!"

Both teams continued cheering for him as his time on first came to a close. He started hustling back to the dugout when Sam walked over and handed Josiah the game ball. The players and coaches kept clapping, and Josiah became the man of the hour.

The game ended, and Josiah was one for one in his Little League debut. After the final out was made and the teams gave high fives to each other, Josiah sat down on the bench and pulled his hat down over his face, a stream of tears running down the sides of his nose. Sam saw the entire thing and squatted down to lift Josiah's hat.

"What's wrong, Josiah?"

Going into this day, we knew it would be his first and last baseball game.

But we didn't know how wonderful the day would be or how Josiah would have so much fun with his new friends. As Josiah walked off the diamond for what we thought would be the last time, he was hooked. This game grabbed him, and it was who he wanted to be. It's part of his identity; he's a ball player. With his head down and tears streaming down his face, Josiah said to Sam, "I don't want it to be over."

Sam pulled us aside and told us what happened. He said he never thought this night would mean so much, not only to Josiah, but also to his team. Then he looked at us and said, "We gotta have another game."

* * *

A few days after the game, Josiah had a stroke.

As happy as those moments at the game were, the consequence was a rude awakening to the life we now had. As much as we felt we were capturing every minute, we were reminded that tomorrow is not promised.

We rushed him to Geisinger Medical Center, and a CT scan showed a CVA, cerebral vascular attack, and for the next day, Josiah lay motionless. Doctors managed to get his eyes open and keep him stable; however, the damage was worse than we expected.

He was paralyzed.

He couldn't walk, couldn't talk. His mouth opened, and you could see him trying to force words out, but nothing happened. It pained us to see him get frustrated, not knowing why his mouth kept opening but no sound would come out. After every couple tries, he just stopped, and all he could do was cry.

Jen held him in her arms with tears running down her face and kissed her little boy, whispering that it was OK. Once again, she was holding onto her heaven as it was slowly slipping away.

It was scary, and after making so much progress medically, spiritually, and together as a family, it was one of the hardest setbacks we had ever had. We were not invincible anymore, and Progeria made that known.

Progeria takes children as early as six to eight years old on incidences similar to Josiah's, so the uncertainty in the hospital became immeasurable. Josiah still couldn't talk. It felt like we lost part of him that day and just didn't know what was next.

We understood he was on borrowed time, and we didn't know how much more his heart could take. Our minds slipped to the worst. Maybe that was it; maybe the Little League game was his big moment and now the worst was coming.

He was stable enough, the doctors said. He wasn't thriving, but there wasn't anything else those hospital walls could do, so they told us to take him home.

No one really knew how long he would last, or how to guide him back to health, but we just prayed he could talk again. His little voice is something we all hold dearly. It's just a muffled chirp that seems to get lost on its way out of his voice box, but it's delicate, and can make the strongest of men smile at their weakest moments. It's part of who he is, and it's our gateway to the joy in his heart. And it was taken away. Selfishly, we wanted it back. We needed it back.

The anxiety set in, and we kept thinking, *This very well could be it. This is the end of what Progeria has given* us. It became a reality we had to face.

But every time Josiah is challenged by defeat, he comes charging back to health.

After only a couple days, he started getting better.

His legs twitched, arms bounced, and he started to look much healthier. Then, after only a few more days, the stroke had resolved itself and his voice came back. He began making sounds. It may not have been the words and sentences he was trying for, but it was so wonderful to hear his voice again. We listened to Josiah's voice like we were hearing him for the first time, and we knew he was not done fighting.

This was a message that this little boy would not give up. Josiah was not done.

With a rejuvenated spirit, knowing this little man was still fighting, it was back to baseball and we would not stop him. We wanted him to enjoy life, and although we didn't know how much time he had left, he was going to have fun with every minute of it.

With every turn, Josiah shows us that he is the miracle God gave to us, and this was no different. This was Josiah's message to us that he would never give up.

Quality over quantity.

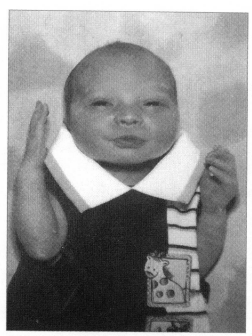

At birth, Josiah looked like a healthy baby boy.

Josiah and his mommy.

Daisha and Josiah ready for school!

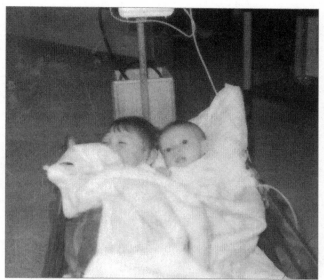

During the darkest moments in the hospital, sometimes the only ray of hope we'd find was in the smiling faces of Daisha and Josiah in this red wagon.

Jen, Daisha, and Josiah having a ball at our local amusement park.

Josiah and his teammate, Chris Rivera, joking around before the game in 2016.

Josiah taking his famous batting practice with Mitch Harris and the 2013 State College Spikes.

Josiah and his good friend and manager, Oliver "Ollie" Marmol, after throwing out the first pitch.

One of our first-ever Spikes games!

Josiah signing autographs with the team!

We still cannot find the words to thank our friend and sponsor, Andy Long, from W & L Subaru, for all he has done for our family.

Joe Putnum and Josiah hard at work chatting over the air on their segment "Action Innings."

First time at Busch stadium in 2014. Josiah being honored on the field.

Family photo of Jen, Josiah, Liz, and Daisha.

Daisha, Josiah, and co-author Dave Bohner grabbing a bite to eat before a Spikes game.

A family photo of Jen, Liz, Daisha, Josiah, and our two dogs Angeline and Scooby.

Game ready!

Daisha and Josiah fast asleep on our way home from the 2014 NYPL Championship game.

Josiah coaching the ESPN *E:60* team at the Travis Roy Foundation Wiffleball Tournament in Essex, Vermont.

Josiah where he belongs. On the dirt of a diamond.

In the dugout with the 2015 Spikes vs. the Staten Island Yankees.

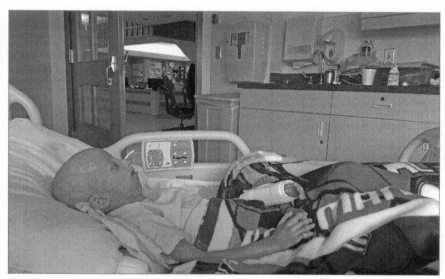

The strongest person I know.

Co-author Jake Gronsky and Josiah at Cardinals Spring Training in 2016.

Josiah displaying the very first shirt from his "Never Give Up" line of t-shirts by Threading Love.

18

FRIENDS FOREVER

"THEY'RE WHAT?" I SAID to Jen in shock.

"ESPN wants to do an *E:60* on Josiah. They're coming to the game!" she shouted once more.

I couldn't believe it.

A few weeks ago, when our Bubby was in a hospital room unable to speak, Coach Sam worked like crazy sticking to his promise of giving Josiah another game, and now ESPN wanted to cover it.

Before we got ahead of ourselves, we needed to clear this with Dr. Walsh. Vigorous activity could possibly trigger another stroke, and no one really knows how a Progeria child will respond. Baseball was no longer an overprotective worry, but a genuine fear. So no matter who wanted to cover the game, we had to make sure it was cleared by our physician and friend.

Jen called Dr. Walsh and they both were in agreement: Josiah needed to be a kid. As scary as it was, he needed to experience life, and we needed to let him do that—no matter the risk.

* * *

In the last week of May, Josiah played a few more games with the Tri-Valley White Sox and was scheduled to finish the last game of the season with his team. But this was different. The local paper had written a heartwarming story about Josiah's first Little League game, and the article rattled through the state. It caught the attention of regional media outlets, and a lot of our Hegins friends began to share the story. One of the people who read the story was the mother of Ben Houser, lead producer of ESPN's *E:60* series.

Ben is originally from the Hershey, PA, area, where his mother and father presently reside. Ben's mom called him and said, "You have to read this article. You are going to want to do a story."

Within the hour, Ben was on the phone with Jen.

Word kept spreading about this little boy's love for baseball, and almost a thousand people alongside ESPN, ESPN's *E:60* film crew, newspapers, and a local radio station airing the play-by-play across their network all showed up to watch Josiah's last game of the season.

But there was one more surprise for Josiah.

Sam's wife and Jen ordered two hundred Little League t-shirts and had "Friends Forever" printed on the back. At the time, they thought they would have plenty of shirts to sell and couldn't wait to surprise Josiah. But within the first ten minutes of warm-ups, the shirts sold out, and the people kept coming. Hundreds more poured into the complex and lined the field. The final day of Little League was now a town celebration.

* * *

It went all day and all evening with only one purpose in mind: to play an inning of baseball with Josiah. We knew a handful of people would show up, but we didn't expect to see the sheer volume of fans that came. We never imagined anything like it, and the love and admiration our family received that day was a moment I will never forget.

Josiah came up for his last at-bat of the night, and he was exhausted. The lights beamed toward home plate, and as the PA announcer called him up to bat, the cheers from the outfield made Hegins Little League feel like Yankee Stadium. He dragged his bat behind his little cleats with the biggest smile on his face, and the dugout started chanting, "Hit-the-ball, hit-the-ball."

At this point, Josiah was so tired he could barely hold his bat, but he would never admit it. Two taps on the plate and he was set for the pitch. Sam, wearing his new "Friends Forever" t-shirt, was on a knee ready to flip. The ball came in, and Josiah took a swing.

Ping! Josiah connected, and the ball trickled off his bat. It dribbled toward first, and Josiah ran down the base path. He pumped his arms and legs as fast as he could and reached first base through an orchestra of cheers. He rounded first and started digging around the bases. The cheers got louder as he crossed each base, and you could see it give him a little extra strength to carry on. Tired and exhausted, he hit home plate, and he was on cloud nine.

Josiah's night ended, and he walked toward the dugout with no tears this time, just a genuine happiness and one big smile. The game was over, but the crowd wouldn't leave. Almost every fan remained in the outfield and just would not go home.

Something held these people there, and as the lights cut through the night, this game became more than baseball.

Fans, coaches, and players started cheering again looking for one last curtain call by the man of the hour. It was our first surreal moment on a baseball diamond. *Is this actually happening?* He was really on the radio. ESPN was *really* here. And now they *really* were staying to cheer on our little boy.

The town remained in the outfield.

We still didn't know what to do, so Jen picked Josiah up and walked around the entire warning track, giving high fives and thanking every fan for showing up. People started thanking Josiah and telling him he was their hero. And it was not sympathetic or patronizing; it was how they felt at that moment, and we were honored.

It finally hit me that all these people were gravitating to the story of a little boy who just wouldn't give up, and I started to wonder, where would it go from here? We weren't looking for popularity or notoriety—we were actually scared of the camera—but was this it? Was this now Josiah's last moment in the sun before he left this world?

And if it were, I would be OK with that. It was a harsh and beautiful realization: Josiah lives a happy life and the time we've spent together will always conquer the time apart. Josiah had so much fun playing baseball with the friends he loves; we didn't need anything more.

He was happy, and that's all we ever wanted.

19

PROFESSIONAL DEBUT

I N 2013, OUR GOOD friends at the Children's Miracle Network invited us to a baseball game. The State College Spikes, the Class A Short Season Minor League affiliate of the St. Louis Cardinals, were having a CMN fundraiser on a Friday night, and our Miracle Sponsor thought it would be perfect for Josiah to be there. By this time, the *E:60* story "Josiah's Time," documenting his now famous Little League game, had traveled throughout the country and became one of the most popular segments on ESPN. And since everyone knew how much Josiah loved baseball, it seemed like a great night for Josiah to meet the team and enjoy some Minor League Baseball.

Fans started pouring into the stadium. The Friday night matchup to begin a new home series packed the place, and every spring-loaded plastic chair was now filled as the stadium swirled with anticipation and 80s rock. They gave us field-level seats just to the right of home plate—five rows up—for the perfect view of Medlar Field.

Built only a few years ago, the state of the art stadium was—and still is—one of the nicest ballparks in the New York-Penn League. I looked around at the beautiful brick and stainless-steel structure giving a modern take on the traditional ballpark and could not help but be in awe. My eyes wandered higher to a major-league style press box and luxury suites wrapping around the back of the stadium while lights sprouted from the rooftops, ready and waiting to cut through the thick summer air and flood the park for the picture-perfect night of baseball.

It was breathtaking, and as the grounds crew manicured and watered the playing surface until not one blade of grass was out of place, for some reason, it felt like ours.

* * *

2013 TEAM

About a week before the Children's Miracle Network fundraising night, the new manager of the Spikes, Oliver Marmol, received an email saying Josiah Viera would be an honorary guest for that evening's game and asked if the team would be able to sign a few autographs before the game. He said that Josiah's name seemed oddly familiar, so he typed "Josiah Viera" into his search engine and found an *E:60* video, "Josiah's Time," about a special night at the Tri-Valley Little League complex in Hegins, Pennsylvania.

He watched the story, and Ollie was speechless. He thought about this story and Josiah's message to never give up, and Ollie knew his team needed to watch it as well.

Maybe it was the intensity of a baseball coach who believed Josiah's story could inspire his young players, or maybe it was a mentor who believed this story was bigger than baseball. For whatever reason—and maybe even a little of both—that next week, Ollie called a meeting.

He gathered the team around the clubhouse television and played the video. Some saw the story before, and some were seeing it for the first time; but as the video ended, the room fell silent. The story touched each player, and the joyful smile of a special little boy captured the hearts of everyone in that clubhouse.

One of the players moved by the story, Mitch Harris, a pitcher for the Spikes who went on to make his major league debut in the next two seasons, stood up.

"We gotta do something special for this kid."

The team agreed they needed to make this day more memorable than just signatures on a baseball. Any child who came to the park could get auto-graphs, and after just a ten-minute video, they knew Josiah was not just any kid. But in the heat of their debate, Ollie looked at the clock and said, "Well, you guys better think of something quick because I'm about to bring him here in five minutes."

* * *

While the Spikes were watching Josiah's *E:60*, which had rapidly become one of the most popular *E:60* videos ESPN had produced up to that point, the Spikes' general manager, Jason Dambach, had met us at the front gate, and we walked to his

office. A towering man in business casual attire, at least six foot
two with a strong face and broad smile, JD welcomed us with his
firm handshake and charming personality. He was down to earth,
a blue-collar worker in slacks, and as we stepped into his office, I
couldn't help but get excited for the day ahead.

Through the glass doors we saw a man approach the room. We
thought it was a coach—or maybe a player—and Josiah waited on
pins and needles to see if this was the manager—if this was our
manager—of his newly found favorite team, the State College Spikes.

The double-click of the push-bar rattled through the room,
and the team's manager, Oliver Marmol, walked through the
door and introduced himself to everyone. He's a charismatic, en-
thusiastic man with the type of personality you'd hope to see in
a leader. Being only in his mid-twenties and of Latin American
heritage, Ollie has an intriguing mix of youth and culture—so
intriguing you'd believe he was still a player.

After we got to know our new manager, it was time for Josiah
to meet the team. We walked through the clubhouse and stopped
at two doors with big Spikes logos and a plaque noting the entrance to the players' locker room. Ollie went in first to make sure
no one was changing or blasting inappropriate music, then yelled
in Spanish to make sure no Latino players were doing the same.
For such a young manager he was quite impressive. He reopened
the door and waved us through.

And the team swarmed us.

The first person to run over and greet Josiah was an older
man who I initially thought was one of the coaches. He shook my
hand then squatted down to meet Josiah with the biggest grin on
his face—other than Josiah's, of course.

"Hey buddy, I'm Mitch Harris," he said opening his hand to
get a handshake. "It's an honor to meet you finally." Little did
we know that moment would start a friendship that soared far
beyond the game of baseball. From the phone calls when Josiah
is sick, to texts on his first days of school, Mitch is truly a great
person inside and out.

Mitch took a photo with Josiah and talked to me for a while
as every player introduced himself to Josiah. Our little man loved

every second of meeting the team and even began joking around with some of the players like they had known each other for years.

We zigzagged around the clubhouse, dodging chairs and tables overflowing with playing cards, and I couldn't help but stare at the crisp uniforms hanging in each locker. The red and blue with the highlight of gold gave each jersey a professional look that I couldn't help but admire, and like a row of red Ford Mustangs, polished and perfectly lined up on a showroom floor, I could only imagine owning one.

After our tour of the clubhouse, we walked toward Ollie's office. It was a small cement cube secluded from the adrenaline-filled chaos of the players' locker room. A desk anchored the room as a small television buzzed in the background—the stereotypical office of Minor League Baseball. We sat down, and Josiah climbed up on my lap. Ollie told us they watched the *E:60* as a team and couldn't have been more inspired to give Josiah a special day at the park. We spoke about life, Josiah's journey, and his love for baseball, and Ollie was glued to every word. There's always a special connection between people and Josiah, but it seemed like Ollie understood, or at least saw the greater purpose Josiah has inside. And I knew right then Ollie would be more than just a coach; he would be a friend.

Fifteen minutes before game time, we headed to the field for Josiah to throw out the ceremonial first pitch. Standing in front of four thousand fans, the PA announcer called Josiah to the mound, and he fired in a strike—well, a strike to any loving parent—to a standing ovation. I looked around at all the smiling fans in the park and realized this place was special. The fans were rowdy and full-hearted, the team was focused and alive, but mostly, there was just something about that place that made me think Josiah belonged.

As fans found their seats and Billy Joel music turned into a pregame pump-up mix, we said our good lucks and ventured down to our field-level seats and settled in for the start of the game. If Josiah wasn't stealing a few sips of my soda or grabbing a bite of his new favorite ballpark food, cheese fries, he was standing on my lap, cheering as loud as his little lungs could push. Then, late in the game, the Spikes tied the score and our hearts thumped with every play.

In the bottom of the ninth inning, the game remained tied. With each pitch, the players shouted and jabbed at the other team as the tension thickened. The other team became a despicable nemesis, and with each strike call, the umpires seemed to end their neutrality and team up with the enemy—or so the dugout assumed. We heard every sudden clap and baseball chatter of "Let's go!" and "Hey, kid!" and any other thought that jolted through their testosterone-fueled minds. Josiah was on the edge of his seat. He mimicked the dugout and chirped for the batter at the plate. Then, with one out, a single shot through the infield— and the Spikes won!

The dugout stormed the field and celebrated a much-needed victory as the night's hero was doused in Gatorade and sunflower seeds—I guess it was the players' customary celebration. The same pump-up mix that started the game was now blaring through the speakers as the fireworks cut through the hazy summer night. It was the perfect end to a perfect night.

But the celebration was not over.

As the fireworks display concluded, JD took us down to the warning track one last time to congratulate the team. But as the players saw their new fan jumping and cheering in front of the dugout, they ran over to us and carried Josiah back to home plate. At this point, fans started to gather their belongings and head home after an electrifying win, but before they could make it to the stairs, they saw a little boy standing at home plate with an imaginary bat in his hands, ready to take a swing as the team cheered him.

He was ready for the pitch.

Mitch Harris stood halfway between the mound and home plate and checked the imaginary runner at second, and two other players squatted behind Josiah to be the catcher and umpire.

The fans saw something more than a win, and they started to cheer. To our surprise, every player on the team huddled around home plate shouting and laughing with anticipation for the big pay-off pitch.

Mitch wildly kicked his leg in the air and pretended to fire a pitch toward Josiah.

Without hesitation, Josiah took a mighty swing and took off for first base. The team went crazy, and the fans followed suit. He pumped his arms and kicked his legs down the line toward first base as the park began to cheer like they did in the ninth. These bases were farther than the ones on his Little League field, so you could see him start to tire halfway down the base path, but it didn't stop him.

He reached first and regained his breath.

But the team kept going wild and cheering for him to round first and head for second; so Josiah did just that. He rounded second and pushed all the way toward third, and the fans came alive. A player simulated being a third base coach, waving him around the plate to score, and the stadium pushed him the rest of the way.

He rounded third, and the team circled around the plate ready for another big celebration. Out of breath and exhausted, Josiah jumped on home plate, and the team lifted him on their shoulders to a thunderous crowd. The crowd drowned out the Billy Joel set list, and the players carried Josiah on their shoulders as the new man of the hour.

A few days later, the story of a little boy's impromptu home run trot that brought a stadium to their feet made the front page of the local paper as an "inspiring few minutes," and a night no one would forget.

*   *   *

That night there was something special that couldn't be explained. This was the start of something much more than just a game, and the team noticed it. There was a burst of energy when most nights a late-inning win would have subsided to a wish. There was something more than baseball here.

That night there was a ray of hope.

Maybe it was the walk-off win and the realization that a playoff push was on the horizon, or maybe it was a little boy who showed each player how important this game truly could be. Whatever the answer, the team had the right combination, and they weren't about to mess with it.

Josiah's high was wearing down, and he was starting to crash. Exhausted and beat, we started gathering our belongings. Before I could lift Josiah and get into the aisle, Ollie stopped us and asked if we'd like to come back.

Josiah caught wind of the invitation and perked up like he did in the ninth.

"Yeah, let's come back, Pappy!" he squeaked.

With a laugh and a smile, I racked my brain, trying to remember our schedule, "Umm. Next Friday?"

Without any debate, Ollie confirmed, and with a handshake and a smile he said, "BP 2:30, see you there."

We were resigned.

The next week we went to the park for another game. This time Josiah was in his full Little League uniform for batting practice and hung out in the clubhouse learning how to play the card game Big 3 with his new team. The stadium and clubhouse workers were getting used to us riding their elevator and no longer asked where we were trying to go. We just got on the elevator and went to the clubhouse. The game started, and we headed to our seats. After a full eight innings, the Spikes went into the bottom of the ninth, and the game remained tied.

And the Spikes won again on a walk-off single.

And Ollie invited us back for a third game.

And the Spikes won again . . .

The team had snapped out of their mid-summer slide and was now in playoff contention. This phenomenon was no longer a question; Josiah was part of a winning streak. For whatever reason or whatever inspiration, the team rallied around this little boy, and Ollie wasn't about to let that go unnoticed. After the third win with Josiah in the clubhouse, Ollie walked up to us and thanked me once again, but I couldn't accept another thank you, as these nights meant the world to Josiah and the pleasure was all ours.

But Ollie insisted.

He saw that this was no longer a charity event. The jerseys were already raffled off the first night and the donation was already made; this was something else. In those three games, Josiah brought something to the team that Ollie couldn't help but notice. It was special, and it was no accident.

As the last day at the park came to a close, Josiah and I said our goodbyes and headed toward the elevator. Josiah ran over to every player to give his last handshake and told them, "Keep playing hard!" As we left the clubhouse, Ollie looked at his team grinning from ear to ear, and as we later found out, he then told himself: *We need to get that kid a locker and jersey.*

From that year on, I think Josiah and I both knew this was a new beginning. This was Josiah's new home.

* * *

"At first people thought we would be doing something great for a little boy, and they were absolutely wrong. He's done a lot for us, and having him in that clubhouse is very important to me."

—2013-2014 Manager of the State College Spikes, Oliver Marmol

20

JOSIAH'S IMPACT: 2014 SPIKES

I T WAS 2014 AND our lives were now at a new start. Just as my family—our struggles, our relapse of pain and walk toward faith—had two beginnings, so did Josiah, and so did his story. When the coma took hold of Josiah in 2005, his first story was one of death. It was a story that slipped beyond the grasp of life and made us realize that even an innocent child is not exempt from the harsh realities of dying. But Josiah never had a choice. His first story was one of inherited struggle and destined grace.

Josiah's second story is one of life.

It's a story that tangibly shows that a miracle life is not one of medical mystery, but one that proves to humanity that love will always conquer pain and life will forever outstretch the hand of death.

And Josiah *does* have a choice in this narrative.

Every day Josiah chooses to go to the baseball field and be the shining example of pure joy. His smile and his happiness have impacted so many people over the years that his story could not be simply be told from a family member's perspective but also must be conveyed by the players who have been inspired by Josiah the most.

These stories belong to them—Josiah's teammates and his friends.

* * *

NICK THOMPSON

June 12th meant forty rounds had come and gone and the St. Louis Cardinals had completed their newest draft class. Forty childhood dreams turned into realities; and forty players solidified their names in local legend immortality before embarking on their first stop on their big-league dream at Short-Season A ball.

The St. Louis Cardinals have four different Short Season A affiliates: The Dominican Summer League Cardinals, specifically for their young international prospects; the Gulf Coast League Cardinals, the first rookie ball affiliate; the Johnson City Cardinals, the Advanced A ball affiliate; and the State College Spikes, the Short Season A ball affiliate. Even though they are four individual teams, they all have the same inherent purpose: develop young talent. Each player's first season in professional baseball is an important stage in development, and these teams act as the incubators for the rest of the full season rosters and, ultimately, the big leagues.

* * *

Day two of the 2014 MLB Draft was about to begin, and Nick Thompson hung up the phone with a scout from his family's favorite organization, the Baltimore Orioles. It was his second of many calls in the day that would change his life forever. "Sixth round, Mom," he said repeating what the scout told him. "That makes the Mets and your precious Orioles both in at rounds five through seven." She put her hands over her heart as if Nick had given her the greatest news in the world and told him, "I'm just so proud of you, hun."

The junior out of William and Mary College was one of the top hitters in the country. From homeruns, to extra base hits, and even leading the country in runs scored, the interesting mix between on-base percentage and power had jumped Nick to the top of many draft boards as the June draft rapidly approached. On that day, it was no surprise his mother was excited because she had been there every step of the way and fell in love with the game the moment her son did.

When Nick was six years old, the local college, Virginia Wesleyan, had their annual Sunday baseball clinics, and he couldn't wait to start playing his newly found love. But as the highly anticipated day came to enroll in his beloved baseball camp, Nick was too young. After all of his anticipation, it looked as though Nick would have to wait another two years before making the required eight-year-old cutoff.

Crushed after hearing the verdict, Nick ran to his mother and buried his face in her hip, but Mrs. Thompson was not going to let some made-up age requirement stand between her son and the game he loved. After reading the camp registration Mrs. Thompson noticed a specific detail that was left undetermined: an age maximum. The camp newsletter clearly stated that all prospective players must be over eight years old, and so after finding a solution to all their problems, she grabbed a pen and scribbled through the signup sheet. They headed home, and Mrs. Thompson looked down at her son wiping tears from his eyes and said, "Get ready, Nick. Tomorrow you're going to baseball camp!"

Trembling with excitement, Nick's anticipation of the camp he had been obsessing over overrode the begging question, how did he get approved? But technicalities were the furthest from his mind. As camp day arrived, he sat on the top of the stairs with his brand-new mitt and baseball uniform he had been wearing for the past week, just waiting for his mother to click on his seat belt so they could take the short thirty-minute drive to the field.

Nick walked with his mother to sign in, his mom said their last name, and the camp organizers checked the clipboard, and then looked at Mrs. Thompson. With eyebrows raised, double-checking the camps regulations, the organizers begrudgingly nodded them through the gates and Nick thought he was officially starting baseball camp. But as roll call started and names were rattled off a list forming the working groups, it was not the name "Nick Thompson" that was expected, but rather "Diane Thompson" that was called to group four. With even more raised eyebrows from the other puzzled parents sitting on the bleachers beyond the chain-linked fence, she grabbed her mitt—along with Nick—and jogged to her group to begin stretching.

Mrs. Thompson told the organizers it just so happened that she was the one wanting to learn the ins and outs of the game (after all, she did play in an adult fast-pitch softball league) and her son just wanted to tag along. There she was, a forty-five-year-old mother in a stretching line of all eight-year-olds doing warm-ups, running poles, and playing second base in a T-ball game just so her son could attend the camp he was wildly dreaming about.

But this was more than just baseball. With every groundball she attempted and every swing she took, Nick knew his mother loved him with her whole heart and this was just a small mile she was willing to run.

*   *   *

Fast-forward sixteen years; the draft had started, and Nick was huddled around a computer with his mother and father watching all the names roll across the screen. They all knew Nick had dreamt of this moment ever since he was a boy attending baseball camp, so the thick silence in the room put the anticipation at an all-time high. Not expecting a call until around the sixth round, Nick was surprised when his phone rang midway through the fourth round.

It was a number he didn't recognize and knew it couldn't be the Mets or his mother's choice, the Orioles.

"Nick, its Matt Blood from the St. Louis Cardinals. Our pick is coming up in round four—will you take sixth-round slot money?"

Slot money is like the price tag at a department store. A first-round pick will be listed with the most expensive price, and every descending pick down to the fortieth round will reflect their suggested price. However, like bargaining for a sale, during the negotiation process, teams will ask if draft prospects are willing to take a lower slot—allowing their t-shirt to be sold on discount.

Sometimes it plays to a player's favor by boosting draft stock to a higher round, and although signing for less money than their projected slot, ultimately they would be gaining more money and leverage through a higher round.

He turned to his mother across the table.

"Mom, they offered sixth-round money," he said hesitantly to his mother, knowing they told every team he filled out questionnaires for or personally worked out for that he would remain firm on slot.

They paused to think. Weighing the pro of a "sure" selection versus the potential of more money if selected by the Mets or the Orioles in the sixth round or earlier was no trivial task. Ultimately, Nick and his mom decided that he would be a man of his word and would have to pass on the offer.

The uncertainties he heard in his mother's voice were enough. He told the Cardinals "No," and the left-handed pitcher, Austin Gomber, was taken by the Cardinals seconds later. Interestingly enough, Gomber signed in the fourth round, so there is no certainty that Nick would have been selected even if he had agreed to take less money.

With the Cardinals' pick, the fourth round was over.

Nick and his parents returned to silence.

His heart thumped in his throat. The draft continued, and his name was nowhere to be found. The moment he hung up the phone, his draft stock plummeted.

The fifth round came, and Nick received a call from his local Orioles scout informing him that he thought they were going to select Nick—but they took a pitcher instead.

Then the sixth round came, and the local Orioles scout again informed Nick he believed the Orioles were going to select him—but they took another pitcher.

The seventh round came, and the same result.

Surely, he would be taken by the eighth round, so Nick eagerly awaited a call from his Orioles scout to end the silence that had been haunting the room. However, both the Mets' and the Orioles' picks came and went, and Nick's name was yet again lost.

Frustrated at this point, Nick knew he made a grave mistake and his mind began to swirl: *Slot money was gone. Maybe I missed my shot. Will my name even be called today? Will I even be drafted?* With each pick that passed by, his living room got a little bit quieter, and finally, to break the silence, he headed back upstairs just to escape and wash away his disgust. As he got to his bathroom, heated up the water, and was about to hop in the shower, the phone rang again. It was the St. Louis Cardinals.

"Nick? This is Matt Blood again. We're going to take you in three picks."

Relieved and elated, he left his bathroom and went to his room to listen to his name be called, as every kid dreams of doing.

"With the 255th pick in the 2014 first-year-player draft, the St. Louis Cardinals select Nick Thompson, right fielder from the College of William & Mary."

As the congratulations texts rolled in, the mood seemingly should have lifted, but the eighth round sounded more like a downgrade, and Nick started to get extremely irritated. He was projected much higher than falling to the eighth round, and their mistake could have cost him a six-figure loss. He still felt the need to rinse away his frustration, so he went to the bathroom without even going downstairs to celebrate and embrace his parents. During his shower, his father knocked on the bathroom door to congratulate him, and instead of accepting the praise Nick replied, "Go away!"

When he finally went back downstairs, Nick continued to push away from his family and even broke away from his mother's hug.

"I turned down the fourth round, Mom." He started to raise his voice. "Now I have to take eighth round slot instead of fourth and there's nothing we can do about it. It's your fault!"

Sharp and cold, Nick's words sliced through the celebration, and the room fell back to the thick silence it once contained. Nick's mind was made up. He turned away from his mother, and he stormed back to the bathroom to just be alone.

He cooled off. He walked to his room, and his mother was sitting on his bed. Tears came to her eyes as she apologized for ruining Nick's day. Hearing his mother cry made him realize how ignorant and nasty he had been toward the people he loved.

"Mom, no, I'm sorry, I was stressed and took it out on you. But there's no excuse. Honestly, Mom, I can't be happier, this is the best day ever!" he said trying to make up for his outburst.

She kept crying.

"Nick, I just wanted you to be drafted by the Orioles."

Letting out a small sigh, he sat down next to her.

"Me too, Mom, me too. But the Cardinals will be great!" he said trying to gently lift her spirits.

"I just wanted you to be close to home, you know."

He put his arm around her, "I know, Mom, me too. But the Cardinals' AA and AAA are less than a day's drive away, and hopefully with a few good seasons I'll be there before you know it!"

But his touch made her cry even harder. Trying to wipe the tears from her eyes she blurted out, "I just wanted you close this year."

He lifted his arm and was startled by where the conversation was now heading. He recognized a strain in her voice not present before.

"This year?" Nick realized she was no longer talking about baseball and became concerned for what his mother was trying to tell him.

"Wait, what do you mean?"

Sobbing with her head in her hands, Nick's throat tightened.

"Nick, I just want you here, with me."

She picked up her head and looked at her son in a way he had never seen before.

"Mom, what's wrong."

"Nick," she said with tears in her eyes and a sniffle in her voice. "I have breast cancer."

* * *

We kept in touch with our good pal, JD, and in the next few weeks the 2014 season was about to start. JD told us they wanted Josiah at as many home games as possible, and his honorary contract started immediately. For the always-special Opening Day weekend, we traveled back to our favorite stadium. It was as breathtaking as the day we left it, but now the prospect of spending the entire season there made this place truly feel like home.

We met JD at the park, and Josiah could barely stand still as it was killing him to be away from the players. Realizing Josiah only wanted to be with his teammates, JD looked at Josiah and sarcastically shot him a grin. "Well, are you finally ready to see your team?"

Josiah put his hands on his hips giving JD the stink eye and jokingly gave a sassy response back, "Yea-ah. Let's go-oo."

We headed to the elevator and got ready to see our new pals. The elevator dinged, and Josiah hurried onto the platform as if to rush the elevator down the shaft. The elevator began its slow descent, and Josiah moved directly in front of the doors to get a head start on the rest of us. As the doors opened, Josiah ran off the elevator and a player from the 2013 team saw him from the hallway and yelled, "JOSIAHHH!"

Whatever conversation had been taking place now stopped, and Chase Raffield, newly signed to the Spikes, was taken aback by this little boy in an oversized Cardinals hat. Of course, he could see Josiah was different; he looks different, walks different, talks different. But there was something else about Josiah that made him different, and Chase couldn't take his eyes off him.

As Josiah hobbled around to fearlessly jump through a crowd of new ball players and introduce himself to each and every one, Chase saw his knees bulging in directions that made him cringe. He looked at this little boy's face and saw the withering age of an old man. But as Josiah hopped around the room with the zest and excitement rivaled by no one, he saw the smile of a child who was not just different, but extraordinary.

The pain and fragility Chase initially saw was triumphed by an inherent joy, and with every flash of his glimmering smile, the team lit up and couldn't help but see the joy God has placed in this little boy's heart.

The team swarmed Josiah, and every player came up for a high five and an introduction. Josiah loves meeting new players, and I could tell this group was special. But before we could do anything else, there was a person we had to see again: our good friend Ollie. We headed to his office.

JD knocked on his door and pushed it open without needing a response. Ollie looked up and saw us and jumped out from his desk.

"Josiah! Welcome back, buddy!" With a big hug, the two reconnected and wasted no time by talking about the upcoming season. Ollie told him the prospect of another playoff run but Josiah was uninterested. He looked at Ollie, and without accepting any other answer he said, "I want a championship."

* * *

CHASE RAFFIELD

The team began to take shape and a new player finishing his college season arrived at the park to get settled into his new locker. A strong hitting outfielder from Cochran, Georgia, Chase Raffield began his professional career with little hype and little expectation after being selected deep within the thirty-second round. But he's a country-strong kid with a southern charm, and being overlooked in the draft just added fuel to his fire.

Growing up in the farmlands of Georgia where the hot sun makes the air heavy and the people tough, Chase was passed over in high school and didn't receive baseball scholarships. He enrolled in a local junior college, and at the open try-out he attended, the baseball team took a chance on him. After two stellar seasons at Lakewood County College—and the growth spurt he was waiting for—Chase accepted a baseball scholarship to play Division I baseball at Georgia State. It was a dream come true, and his hard work finally started to pay off.

But just as quickly as he committed, he tore his ACL and imagined the worst. An outfielder with a torn ACL is no use, and it would be a waste of scholarship money. He called his coach, told him the news, and braced himself. But the head coach told him there was a reason they signed him, and there was a reason they wanted him on campus. To his surprise, they upheld his scholarship.

It became his saving grace, and that leap of faith by his head coach gave Chase the opportunity he was looking for his entire life. Chase went on to be one of the best players in college baseball, and the St. Louis Cardinals selected him late in the 2014 draft.

The draft was over and he was focused on preparing for Opening Day. He completed his physicals, received his team gear—including a bright red body bag, and set up his first-ever professional locker. He was blown away, and Chase quickly realized professional baseball was a lot different than a mid-major baseball program.

Just as a day of meeting coaches and teammates and running around in circles preparing for the season came to a close, Chase walked out of the locker room and took a seat in the clubhouse. As he flipped through the television channels with his new teammates, an elevator door dinged, the doors opened, and a call from the other room of "JOSIAHHH" echoed down the hall. Chase snapped his head around and saw, hobbling through the clubhouse, a little boy with the biggest smile on his face.

* * *

COLLIN RADACK

Later that night, around two a.m. in Chicago International Airport, Collin Radack woke up from his poor attempt at sleep on the hard tile floor. The newly drafted outfielder from Austin, Texas, had been traveling all day—delayed flight from Texas to Charlotte, delayed connecting flight from Charlotte to Chicago, then his final flight of the night from Chicago got cancelled. Nothing short of an airport trifecta. He turned over and rolled his sweatshirt into a ball and shoved it under his neck to try and at least catch a few hours of sleep before another seven a.m. flight, but couldn't help but think this was undoubtedly the worst omen his season in State College could have.

Before being taken in the twentieth round by the Cardinals on day three of the 2014 Draft, the dream of becoming a professional baseball player looked to remain just that for a skinny, under-recruited senior from Cedar Park High School. He was a solid player with good fundamentals but just never had the tools to stand off the page to any recruiter, so when in April of his final marking period of high school, Radack was offered a spot to play Division III baseball at Hendrix College—he jumped on the opportunity for it.

It was no surprise he flourished at Hendrix; he's smart, decisive, and has just a big enough chip on his shoulder to make it interesting. The smaller pond made Collin a bigger fish, and after four years of stellar play in DIII baseball, plus a work ethic that made the once skinny slap hitter into a muscularly built clean-up batter, Collin was selected by the Cardinals but was in for a rude awakening—literally.

His flight from Chicago departed later that morning, and he finally boarded the plane to take him to Philadelphia. After a three-hour bus ride and thirty-three total hours later, Radack was officially at his new home just in time for Opening Day. But the moment Collin stepped on Medlar Field he realized this was no longer Division III baseball and he was rightfully intimidated.

He had no idea what he was getting into and thoughts of "Am I good enough" crept into his mind like the morning after a bad dream. He walked into a clubhouse of players speaking a language he couldn't understand and was thrown right into the mix of players that had been practicing and living together for at least a week. He was the odd man out, and trying to fit in while starting his professional career was quite overwhelming. Collin unpacked his bags and tried to settle in. As he leaned back in his chair he saw Dave and Josiah walk through the hall, and Collin's eyes lit up. "That's him!"

*   *   *

Dave and Josiah headed back for Opening Day weekend. Five thousand people filled the stands on a gorgeous summer night and they settled in for nine innings of baseball. After meeting all the new guys, Josiah noticed a player running over to him with the biggest smile on his face. He looked like a very nice kid—polite, always smiling, but a little sheepish. He walked over and introduced himself as Collin Radack.

Dave noticed there was something different the way this player. Maybe he was a teammate from the year before, Dave thought, but from the way he approached Josiah, it was if he knew him.

There are moments in life when you will never forget exactly where you where, and right as Collin saw Josiah, his mind shot back to a Texas evening in ninth grade. Collin was sitting on his bed just flipping through channels after completing his homework and stopped on an ESPN *E:60* documentary called "Josiah's Time." The story between a little boy's love for baseball and his fight for life simply grabbed him and wouldn't let go. He thought about this little child and a relationship with life and death that he couldn't understand. The idea of God and the special light He gave this little boy stayed with him for days and the dialogue between Tom Rinaldi and Josiah on the topic of Heaven became a verse he couldn't ignore.

"What is Heaven?" Tom asked.

"It's God," young, six-year-old Josiah said in a high-pitched voice, pointing to the sky.

Tom smiled and pointed up to the sky along with his new buddy.

"What do you think Heaven looks like?"

"Jesus."

Collin snapped back to the clubhouse and couldn't believe he was finally with the child from the documentary. For that moment he forgot all about his rocky introduction to professional baseball and started to think maybe this was an even better omen for his season. Superstitions aside, Collin knew he needed to find out more about this little child and why God put them in the same room.

*   *   *

We finished the pregame routine and hung out in the club-house. Trying to remember everyone's names, shaking every-one's hands, and having a full clubhouse of players introduce themselves to our little man usually made my head spin. Sitting down for a few minutes until Josiah's ceremonial first pitch never sounded better. Ever since last year, the Spikes let Josiah throw out the first pitch. It had become routine for the park, and every time his name was called, he fired a first pitch to a standing ova-tion. It was his big moment each night, and he had been looking forward to it since his last pitch in 2013. And like the rest of the players in the clubhouse, he was nervous.

A few minutes later, the fuzzy digital clock above the locker room doors read 6:15, and the clubhouse was thick with an eerie mix of anticipation, concentration, and superstition. Other than the occasional bark of a pump-up one-liner of "Let's GO!" to re-lease the pregame jitters, music was played loud and words were soft. It was Opening Day weekend, and tonight started everyone's professional season, including ours.

6:35 p.m. flicked to the clock, and the team headed out for pregame stretch. With a few bats in hand and a glove cradled in a helmet, the clacking of metal cleats and the crunching of cement filled the dugout. With each step, reality started to set in. This was it. This was Opening Day, and as they got closer, whatever insecurity they had in the clubhouse slowly turned into confi-dence. Their night was about to begin, and above all, it was time to be a kid; it was time to go play.

*   *   *

I joined the band of photographers gathering near the pitcher's mound as Josiah walked over the red-felt carpet stretched across the first baseline before we had to head to our seats for the game. The PA announcer took a deep breath and called "Joo-siahhhh V-iiiii-era-hhhhhh!" to the mound. It was a fresh, springtime sound—like turning over the engine of a Mustang GT for the first time after a long winter in the garage.

Josiah scooted to the mound to applause no less than the same amount of cheers from last year, wearing the same oversized Little League shirt that started his love for the game. He delivered yet another perfect strike that only went a few feet before rolling across the plate, and got a high five from the Spikes player and a picture from the row of paparazzi—including me.

We gave our final good luck to the players and Josiah went down the row for a final pep talk and high fives. We slipped through the dugout one last time and took our seats right next to our team.

It was a perfect night of baseball behind the painted sunset of a June summer sky. And we picked up right where we left off with another Spikes win.

Josiah would stay with the guys all night if he could, but I had to be the bad guy and get him home for his bath before his mom started to worry. The postgame meal died down, and we grabbed some leftovers before the players ran over to say goodbye to their new buddy. Like always, we walked out of the stadium smiling from ear to ear. I strapped Josiah into his car seat, and by the time I closed the door he was out like a light. Five years ago this was a night we never dreamed about, a life we never knew existed, and as I pulled out of the Medlar Field parking lot and saw the hazy lights in my rearview, I couldn't help but smile.

21

THE JERSEY

WE WALKED INTO OLLIE'S office for our daily lunch meeting and Josiah climbed up on his lap. We chatted about the season so far—the dominant pitching, the stellar offensive season by Rowan Wick hitting over .375 with fourteen home runs and slugging .815*, and the adjustments the rest of the team needed to make moving forward. As we were talking, Josiah lifted the lineup closer to his face in order to study it and without hesitation he cut our conversation off and blankly pointed at the bottom of the lineup card.

"Why is he in the lineup, today?"

"Well buddy, at this level of the minor leagues . . ." Ollie delicately tried to explain to Josiah. "Everybody gets a chance to play and move up to the big leagues."

Josiah put the card down in understanding.

"OK?"

"Yeah," Josiah sighed. "But does he have to play today? We really need this win."

Ollie and I howled with laughter, and Josiah reciprocated with a long giggle and a high five to his manager. But from that moment on, Ollie received his first awakening that Josiah was no longer just going to be a spiritual lift for his players; he was now taking on a role in their development.

Josiah knew each guy on a personal level, and he saw how they performed on the field. He understood the banter, the jokes, but he saw the frustration after a tough loss, and he saw the triumphs after a hard-fought victory. And he got to know them

---

* After the 2015 season, Rowan Wick transitioned into a new position and would continue his baseball career in the Cardinals organization as one of the top pitching prospects.

on a professional level—their best skills, their worst fears, their motivation, their execution, even their ability to round first base on a single. He studied the team and studied the game.

But what Josiah couldn't understand was everything the guys saw in him.

They heard his story, they saw his life, but couldn't grasp the happiness that came with such hardship. So, just as Josiah had been watching them, they tried to learn. They looked for why this kid could have so much joy in the face of so much pain and hurt. And they absorbed every bit of happiness that little boy gave to them and filtered it throughout their lives. As much as my little boy loved being around the guys and learning about the game of baseball, Josiah was able to give lessons of life back that the game of baseball could never reach.

* * *

DANNY DIEKROGER

One of the best college seniors in the draft, the first baseman out of Stanford, was selected quickly in the tenth round by the St. Louis Cardinals. A very down-to-earth person with an IQ about twice that of the average baseball player, Danny Diekroger has a mix of brilliance with a Southern California vibe that makes him appear to be the kind of person who ponders Plato's Symposium while surfing the shores of Santa Monica in his spare time. It was only fitting that after his draft selection, Danny had to study for a math final and prepare a computer science project before securing gradua-tion—pushing his Opening Day back a few days.

But this one particular day Danny got to the park a few minutes after 2:30 p.m. for a 3:45 pre-BP stretch, and his buddy Josiah was already waiting for him. Danny swapped out his dress code attire—wrinkled polo shirt, khaki shorts—for his Spikes Dri-Fit shirt, matching BP shorts, and a pair of slide-on sandals. He grabbed a deck of cards, found his new buddy, and in a silly taunt yelled, "All right, JV! I got the cards, and you're going down!"

This playful rivalry started the first time Josiah made his first impression on the newly signed infielder. After Danny completed his schoolwork he flew directly to State College—four games into the season—and picked up his hot hitting right where he left off in college. But as steady as his offense started, the defensive switch to third base was rocky and Josiah took notice to the early errors. So, when Josiah arrived at the stadium, he had a bone to pick with the new third baseman.

The first time Danny saw this little kid with all the players, he was stunned by his stature and couldn't help but notice a certain twinkle in his smile—one that stuck with Danny the first few days at State College. By this time Josiah was already running around the clubhouse, talking to the players and shuffling in and out of Ollie's office like it was his own. The team told Danny about this special little kid—his smile, his laugh, his likeness, and everything that made him a bit more special than everyone else—so Danny was excited to finally get his chance to introduce himself to the kid he had heard so much about.

"Hey, man, my name's Danny," he said to Josiah, getting the standard high five and hug greeting. But before Josiah introduced himself, he put his hands on his hips, and like a concerned parent explaining the obvious rules of a 9:00 p.m. curfew, in his squeaky voice said, "Danny, you're supposed to throw the ball to the first baseman, not over his head."

The clubhouse erupted in laughter, and Josiah cracked a big smile. Danny took the teasing in stride as Josiah got high fives around the clubhouse for giving the new guy a hard time. But from this point on, their teasing rivalry was now ignited, and they made sure to settle it each day over a game of cards.

The July heat began to sink in, and a group of ball players huddled around a batting cage early in the afternoon. The first month of the season had taken a toll on most of the guys, as professional baseball usually does not give easy introductions. Working on their swings and talking about necessary adjustments, the players tirelessly tried to find the right combination of skill and confidence to bring to that night's matchup.

As the sweat poured, the cage rang with baseballs shooting into the back of the net, and the players felt a watchful eye over the crowd of hitters. Without warning the players heard a soft "Good swing" and "Nice one, Danny" from behind the screen. It was Josiah, equipped with his batting gloves and new T-ball bat, just watching and waiting for his turn before mandatory team stretch whisked the guys away.

"JV! C'mon and hit with us, my man," one of the players invited.

"OK, I'll hit after Chase," he said, responding like any veteran ball player would.

Josiah scooted closer to the cage and began keying in on Chase's round. Swing after swing, Josiah focused on how he connected with each baseball.

He was watching, learning, but more importantly, he was filing every bit of information their informal batting practice gave into the back of his mind. Then it was his turn, and he replicated exactly what he had been learning. Danny and Chase stayed to flip to the little man, and without any extra instruction, he hit every single baseball thrown in his direction.

"Same time tomorrow, JV," Danny joked. "This time, don't be late."

They left the cage, and Chase carried Josiah back to the clubhouse so he wouldn't waste any more of his limited energy walking down the long corridor. The four buddies got back to the clubhouse to meet Dave before they had to head toward the field.

*　*　*

Walking to the dugout is always a special feeling. Like butter-flies fluttering throughout our Subaru on the way here, holding my little man as we walk to the dugout is a feeling that Josiah and I will hold forever.

We grabbed his glove and his helmet from his neatly groomed locker and made a sharp left after the trainer's room to reach the declining tunnel where the carpet abruptly turns into rubber matting. Standing at the top of the descent, we looked to the directory plaque that said "To Field" and ventured through. The cement tunnel took us under the stands, and the damp air smelled like the dust of a cellar basement.

We were getting closer.

The sun peeked out the dugout's entrance, and with each step, the distant light became piercing. I put Josiah down and let him run the last few steps. The tunnel opened up to a wide dugout sunken halfway into the ground, wooden plank boards completed the staircase, and we were met by the playing surface of the State College Spikes. Although we have now made this walk hundreds of times, I still get chills as the smell of fresh-cut grass and chatter of a baseball team begin to touch my senses.

We stepped off the stairs, and our shoes crunched over the gavel warning track neatly bordering the freshly cut grass, which looked more like a bright green carpet than rows of sod. Josiah began looking every which way trying to take it all in, and I followed suit.

Screens littered the infield, protecting players from baseballs whizzing by their heads, and the dirt under their feet had just been watered and matted to ensure the perfect ground ball every time. I looked around the stadium and saw the thousands of empty seats being wiped clean in preparation for thousands of fans to soon fill each one. My eyes wandered higher to major-league press boxes and luxury suites wrapped around the back of the stadium and the racks of lights that would soon flood everything below. It was elegant, it was truly a first-class stadium, and for some reason, it felt like it was ours.

*　*　*

COLLIN RADACK

Batting practice came to a close and Dave and Josiah stayed off to the side where no baseballs could reach them. As the last group of hitters completed their round, Ollie signaled from behind the batting screen for Josiah to get ready; he was up.

If you've never seen a professional batting practice, it's more like watching a symphony orchestra than a sporting event. The BP thrower acts as the conductor, setting the tone for each note and keeps the pace for the entire performance.

He waits until the hitter raises his bat then fires the first pitch. The batter swings at the pitch cueing the fungo hitter* to deliver a ground ball to each of the infielders while the outfielders and pitchers gather the struck baseballs. Infielders catch their ground ball and throw to opposing bases in synchronization. By the time the infielder completes the play, the BP thrower is back on his stand ready to deliver the next pitch. The infielders reset and the routine restarts.

It's a fluent performance on the field being accompanied by the background music of the stadium's choice. Hitters then rotate in and out of a shell-like screen over home plate executing a number of hitting drills in order to prepare for the night's game. And as soon as each hitter is done and the last ball is thrown, the players clear the field and the production ends as swiftly as it began.

---

* A fungo hitter is the coach standing off to the side of the cage hitting ground balls usually with a long, skinny baseball bat, known as a "fungo." The special bat gives the coach more accuracy and control to be able to precisely replicate specific plays the infielder would face in the game.

Josiah warmed up to partake in his now-famous walk-off homerun batting practice. It was the highlight to everyone's BP, especially Radack's. His adjustment to professional baseball had been hard. He really hadn't cracked the lineup and spent most of the games just watching, waiting for his name to be called. He was alone, and all the questions of "Am I good enough" had resurfaced, and the game seemed to pass him by. But steadily, Radack began to look forward to batting practice; not for the extra work he felt like he needed, nor the chance to show the coaches his worth, but for a different perspective. Every time this little man walked to the plate, the game that had been spinning around in Radack's mind came to a stop. For ten minutes, Radack could escape reality. For ten minutes, Radack saw something more than a game.

The players jogged off the infield to collect all the baseballs, and Ollie yelled over, "Josiah, you're up!" As the players heard their manager call Josiah to hit, they dropped their baseballs into the bucket and formed a wall around the hitter's shell to get a front-row view. Josiah ran to the plate in his oversized helmet slumping over his face and his T-ball bat bouncing off the ground with every puttering step. He got to the box, tapped home plate twice, and set his hands just like Coach Sam had taught him.

He was ready for the pitch.

The team was getting rowdy from the anticipation of watching this little kid swing a bat just as big as he is, and they started to hoot and holler. The BP pitcher got set and delivered the pitch.

PING!

Josiah hit the first pitch, and it started to make sense to Radack. He remembered the documentary and the perseverance this little guy needed just to survive, and as corny as he thought it was, he thought God put this little boy here on purpose.

The magnitude of playing for the St. Louis Cardinals organization and all the pressures of the game began to take their toll on Radack. But as he continued to watch this little boy's round, the message that God put Josiah here for a reason sank deeper into his heart. With each swing of Josiah's bat, which was almost as tall as Josiah stood, Radack saw the game as it should be: through the joy of one tough little kid. He started to believe this was more than just a batting practice or a fun activity for Josiah; this was his call to have courage.

But Radack wasn't the only one to be moved by Josiah. One of the Cardinals field coordinators was in town making sure everything was running up to standard. He's a proud, barrel-chested man with a loud and intimidating voice that was one of the most respected in the Cardinals organization. Mark DeJohn, or DJ, was stunned by this little boy at home plate.

After watching the team's lethargic round of batting practice compared to Josiah's one hundred percent effort, he began asking questions and finding out who this little boy was. Moved by his story and inspired from his round of batting practice, DJ walked inside the clubhouse and gave every hitter a lesson they wouldn't forget.

He began by talking about baseball, the Cardinals, and what was expected of every player in the organization. He reminded them of the "Cardinal Way," the idea that players wearing the Birds on the Bat must go above and beyond what is expected because the Cardinals do not accept anything less than exceptional.

And then he asked the hitters what they needed to do to get to the big leagues. Players responded with smart, well-versed answers, but DJ didn't accept any of them.

His face remained firm; his chest out, back straight. The players were silent.

DJ pointed toward the field and said they needed to be more like that little boy taking batting practice. He told the team that Josiah has more fight and more tenacity than everyone sitting in that room, and until they could be more like him, the big leagues would be nothing but a dream. DJ left the room and thanked Josiah for being the example the team needed to see. Josiah always grabbed the team emotionally, but now he was the example players needed to follow.

*   *   *

"Di' y'all go inta th' clubhouse yet?" said a tall, stringy pitcher from Alabama with a southern drawl that pulled his Adam's apple up and down like a fishing bobber.

"No, not yet. Why, what's going on?" I asked, hoping nothing was wrong.

"Ohhh boy." He looked at Josiah with a smile. "He's gon' lo-uhh-ve this." He motioned us to the door, and we hustled inside.

The moment we stepped foot inside the locker room the guys were waiting with smiles on their faces. Like we just walked into our own surprise party, the team giggled and nudged us toward the middle of the room. I looked around to see the players laughing and egging us on our wild goose chase, and then my eyes began to fill with tears as I saw a locker with the name "Josiah Viera" hanging from the name tag above.

They got him his own.

My little man went running over with the biggest smile on his face while the team swarmed him. To see Josiah that happy are the moments that will never grow dull and the days that seem to always find their shine even years after the moment passed. But then, I looked into his locker, and I began to get emotional. Hanging on the rack, there was a brand-new, custom-made, official State College Spikes jersey with "Viera" embroidered across the back.

The guys helped him try on his new jersey, and it fit perfectly—well, close enough. They ordered the smallest size possible and had a tailor cut the shoulders in half so his arms could fit through. It was perfect, and he wouldn't take it off. I thanked the team and thanked Ollie a thousand times, but my words fell flat to the gratitude that flooded my heart.

Josiah gave hugs to everyone in the clubhouse in his official jersey and ran over to his locker. They opened his official chair, sat him in front of his official locker, and when his eyes explored his new summer home, his smile said it all.

He was officially a State College Spike.

My feet didn't hit the floor the entire day. Just like the other players had done with their own equipment, I placed his bat, helmet, and glove in the locker and pointed his chair toward his new locker before we headed to the stands for game time. Like usual, JD came down to the clubhouse to bring us to our seats for the game, and I thanked Ollie one last time before he headed down the tunnel. He took a look at JD, then looked at me with a straight face: "Josiah's got his jersey on for the game, right?"

I laughed and nodded at the obvious question.

"Ollie, I think I'm gonna have trouble prying it off him when we leave."

"Great. Well, grab his helmet; we'll see you down there," he said without a chance for rebuttal, and walked toward the dugout.

Knowing what he meant but worried he might get in trouble, I looked at JD. He nodded with a grin and then yelled, "Enjoy the game!" as he headed to the elevator, not letting my conscience get in the way of the moment. Maybe it was the nirvana of Josiah receiving a locker and jerseys coupled with the manager and GM's undisclosed OK, but without hesitation, I stuck Josiah's helmet down past his ears, picked up my little man with the biggest smile yet, and we marched toward the dugout.

22

THE DUGOUT

I DIDN'T KNOW WHAT the reception would be like with the team. I didn't know how the guys would feel about a child and his grandfather hanging around, talking with the guys, and then stepping foot in their dugout. Our excitement to be on the field during a professional baseball game was bursting through our skin only to be held back by the uneasiness that we were somewhere we didn't belong. I stood in the corner, holding Josiah, trying to take up as little space as possible, hoping no one would notice us. But as the players started filing in, my plan was dead in its tracks as they welcomed us like our first day walking through the elevator doors.

This one particular day, Chase and Collin weren't playing, so naturally Josiah climbed up on the wooden bench right next to his buddies, and we were set.

Players were talking baseball with Josiah and giving high fives. He was smiling the entire game. Then as Josiah felt more comfortable in the dugout, he would go up to players and give them a tap on the leg and say "Good job" after a nice play.

He was part of the system—part of the open, explicit dugout that held every bit of emotion to this game. And without a word, Josiah would scoot up the stairs and stand next to his new friend Ollie and gain a few pointers about the game at hand. He loved it; quite frankly, he just blended in.

* * *

Baseball is a game of individual efforts roped together for one goal. Even though the fans see nine position players on a diamond, when a player steps to the plate, he's alone in the spotlight. In that at-bat, the stadium's immediate attention is focused directly on the test between the pitcher and hitter—the cat and mouse game between the game's pitted rivals—and their focus brings judgment. Baseball is a game where failure is more common than success, and each night players are forced to accept the vulnerability the diamond brings. At best, the spotlight feels good and the cheers from the crowd make you feel invincible; and at worst, the spotlight is crippling and a silent crowd after a bad night only magnifies your insecurity. There are times when the game feels too easy and Busch Stadium is only but a slingshot away, while other times the game humbles you and makes you question if you even belong between the lines.

The only refuge a player finds is in the dugout.

It's their protection from the game, a place they can let the game pause for a moment before banging their cleats and going back out. And it's off limits. It's truly the player's territory, and outsiders are not welcome. Most of the time it's fraternity and reflection on the game; but in times of weakness it's self-absorption and insecurity disguised as throwing a helmet with an endless bark of curse words. It's raw, it's uncensored, and it's the recipient of every emotional peak and valley of young adults in their journey to manhood.

*　*　*

Josiah was welcomed like family.

Every game we could make, we arrived promptly at two o'clock p.m. to check in with Ollie and go over the night's game. He always let Josiah see the lineup card and even had him check it for approval before posting it in the clubhouse. After our afternoon lunch, as I called it, we went to see the players as they arrived for early work. Chase, Collin, Nick, and Danny would hurry into the clubhouse to see the little man before their daily routines started. Chase entered the room, and Josiah took off and ran directly into him with the biggest bear hug his little arms could reach.

"My man! Yuh didn't forget, did yuh?" he said in his deep Georgia twang, teasing Josiah to prove he remembered the handshake. Josiah laughed, and through his crackling squeaky voice he said: "No-ooo!" And with a quick rebuttal he stared at Chase, "Did you?"

They stopped the teasing and initiated their handshake. Once it was official and proved they both hadn't forgotten the sacred greeting, Josiah told Chase to join in the next hand of cards and quickly ran back over to his table with Danny, Nick, and Collin knowing if he didn't hurry, he would need to wait until the next game.

It was pushing three o'clock, and pretty soon the players would start heading to the batting cage for some extra work before their 3:45 team stretch. Sometimes all I could do was take a seat and try to soak in these moments given to us. I looked back at our little man, hooting and hollering over a game of cards, and felt a sense of belonging I never thought we would find.

Over the past summer, I got to see our little man make friends with people we used to idolize and dream about meeting. I didn't know how the team would respond to Josiah or if being in the clubhouse would become a nuisance to the players. But each day we were there, the more welcomed we were—and the harsher we were teased for the days we were not. I listened to the game of cards being played in the background and realized the joy that was running through my body was common blood throughout the clubhouse. It was honest and genuine, and as my starry-eyed gaze around the clubhouse came back to reality, I no longer saw my grandson with a bunch of baseball players. I saw a group of friends.

* * *

NICK THOMPSON

Two days after finding out his mother had been diagnosed with breast cancer, Nick had the impossible task of packing everything he could in his high school Passat and driving to State College. He hadn't seen her since the day he said, "I love you," then left, and his mind was anywhere but the diamond.

The first round of chemo came quickly, and Nick was somewhere on the field away from his family. Each day spent with baseball was a day spent away from his mother, and the hours missed by her side were becoming heavy. But the season dredged on and Nick had to keep pushing forward.

A few weeks into the season, Ollie called a team meeting before they left for their road trip, so the team scattered chairs around the clubhouse to get a direct view of their manager. The Cardinal Way—respectful, professional, and engaged at all times. But as the meeting began, Nick clutched to his phone because the next update from his mother's chemo would arrive any minute.

Whatever his manager was saying fell short of his mind, and his eyes darted from his phone's screen, then back to his manager, making the entire meeting a blur. Then finally his phone rang and Nick barreled through the scattered chairs of his teammates and ran to the hallway to answer.

His father told him she was doing fine, and doctors were very optimistic. But his answer was quick, and prepared, almost an introduction to tell him something else. Then he paused.

"She's starting to lose her hair, Nick."

* * *

After the meeting, Nick was called to Ollie's office. Nick never missed a word his manager said, never blatantly broke any rules, and never forgot the Cardinal Way, so rushing out of a meeting was highly concerning to his manager.

He sat down, and Ollie asked him what was going on. He wasn't angry with him or disciplining him, but had genuine concern as to why Nick had been acting so out of character.

Nick had kept his mother's sickness a secret the entire season, but now it was time to come clean. Slouching back into his chair, Nick broke down into tears. He couldn't find the words to explain how much he loved his mother and would do anything to support her, but then turned around and drove four hundred miles to be away from her in the time she needed him the most. He loved his mother more than baseball, yet each day he was choosing baseball over his mother, and that day it had all become real.

He spilled his life to his manager, and they talked for an hour. As Nick pulled himself back together, Ollie looked at him and asked if he wanted a day off to clear his mind. He thought about having a day to regroup and starting fresh tomorrow, but told Ollie, "No, my mother wanted me to come out here and play baseball, and that's what I'm gonna do."

He walked out of Ollie's office and sat at his locker. His head was as clear as it could get so he walked out to the clubhouse to be with the guys. Smiling and giggling at the littlest joke, Nick heard Josiah playing his daily hand of Big Three and was struck by this little boy's happiness.

Josiah had been given the toughest road out of any of the players, yet Nick realized that he was the happiest of them all. Torn by the idea that a child who looked so weak and so unlucky could rise above all limits of human virtue and show such strength, Nick wanted what Josiah already had. He saw the light God placed in such an innocent little boy and started to understand. He looked at Josiah laughing and giggling while barely being able to hold his cards and quietly prayed, "God, give my mother the courage, strength, and resilience of Josiah."

*   *   *

His family bought her a wig the same color of her long flowing brown hair, but she never wore it; she was too proud and too faithful to cover up the badge of honor after her first weeks of chemotherapy. She was weakening by the treatment, but her will remained strong; and the time for a road trip was long overdue.

Wearing a brightly-colored wrap around her head as the universal sign of courage, Mrs. Thompson walked into Bowman Field with her husband to watch their son play against the in-state rivals, the Williamsport Cross-Cutters.

Bowman Field, or now BB&T Park at Bowman Field, is the second-oldest ball park in Minor League Baseball and certainly looked like it. Before the renovations, wooden crates acted as the opposing team's lockers; players had to walk through the fans to get to the field; and home plate was about a football field away from the dugout, making the long walk after strikeouts a miserable journey—the epitome of Minor League Baseball. But fans loved it, and it was the Thompsons' last hope of seeing their son finally bust out of his three-game slide and get a hit.

Already 0-11 coming into this game, Nick was 0-4 on the day, having made the long strikeout journey back to the dugout twice already. With every swing and miss he could feel his parents cringe, knowing his mother would not accept driving all the way from Virginia to watch her son strike out all weekend. Nick told himself to relax and just play the game his mother worked so hard for him to enjoy. Knowing his mother's love for him was beyond a game of baseball, Nick knew that regardless of the outcome, she would always be proud of him. He walked to the plate for his final at-bat of the weekend and crushed the first pitch he saw over the left field wall—his first professional home run. Ironically enough, the home run came on Father's Day.

Rounding the bases, he couldn't help but think about all the home runs his mother was able to watch over the years. From his first baseball camp with his mom by his side to Little League all the way to his last days in college, his mother had been there every step of the way, retrieving every home run ball for their collection at home (although she did have to bribe a kid with $10 to get this ball back, just like she had been known to do in the past). But this one was different. This was the first home run she saw in a professional uniform, and it was one she would never forget.

He touched third and looked to the crowd to find his mother waving her arms and screaming at the top of her lungs. Nick saw her and couldn't help but laugh at her motherly love resonating throughout the old wooden park. He stepped on home plate and now made the long trek back to the dugout, but this time, a celebratory parade. The moment he got to the dugout, Josiah met him at the top step before anyone else, and with arms extended and a big smile he said, "I knew you were gonna do it! I knew it!"

Nick couldn't help but smile. As he looked at Josiah jumping and cheering for his home run he remembered the countless prayers to make his mother more like Josiah. He turned back to his mother in the stands, still jumping and cheering, and knew this was exactly where God wanted him.

After the season, when Nick reflected on his year, neither his personal statistics and success nor the Spikes' championship resounded in his mind. He could not stop thinking about Josiah. In a time where his mother battled through chemotherapy, he had Josiah to remind him of God's goodness and perfection. In a time when his mother could hardly keep food down, he could enjoy cutting up Josiah's food into tiny bites so that his body could handle it. In a time when the oceans seemed the roughest, Josiah served as a constant reminder that God was with him.

* * *

The hours Josiah spent watching games, watching batting practice, and ultimately studying the team, had made him an asset to these players. He started giving tips and observations to the team of what he saw, and no one was safe. Like Josiah checking Ollie's lineup each night, Josiah checked each player—and it was not trivial. When Josiah would go into the cage before BP, he would hound Chase about getting a bigger leg kick before he started his swing to gain more power. How Josiah knew that or even formulated that idea shocked Chase to start, but then as he thought about it—Josiah was right.

So, they worked on it each day in the cage together. Josiah would make sure the pitchers were doing their jobs correctly and would stand behind the mound during a warm-up session. One youngster had a cannon for an arm but just could not throw strikes. Watching him throw for a few minutes with the pitching coach, Josiah told him to straighten his knee before he threw so he could be more accurate. The pitching coach looked at Josiah, then at his young pitcher, and said, "Yes! That will stop your front side from leaking forward; listen to him!"

I guess when Josiah went into the dugout, the team expected it as the natural next step their new coach should take, and they knew his eyes would be on them the entire game.

Josiah continued to give tips and high fives throughout the game and continued his role as the honorary bench coach. He started taping his wrists like the players after they'd put on their game jerseys every day at 6:15—not a minute sooner, not a minute later.

I like to say Josiah was adopted without him knowing it. By the time I let him go from my arms, he was off with his friends, leaving me alone in the clubhouse with the rest of the new rookies. But what I never realized was that the team adopted me, too. I never played baseball before, never watched it consistently, and never would I imagine I would be spending my summers on a professional baseball field, so when the team started calling me "Pap," I started to feel like I belonged as well.

* * *

The team was making another case for playoffs, but Josiah wasn't settling for a playoff spot; he had made it very well known that he wanted a championship. This particular game was crucial to get us into the championship series, but it was slipping away; a late opportunity for the Spikes to take the lead rested on Brian O'Keefe's at-bat. After two questionable calls by the home plate umpire, Brian took a step out of the box. "It was a pivotal situation, and by the death grip around his bat, he knew it.

The next pitch, Brian swung wildly at a high fastball and popped it up to the first baseman. And that didn't sit right with Brian.

O'Keefe is a strong, square-built catcher out of St. Joseph's College in Philadelphia, and he is one of the top catching prospects in the Cardinals system. The sixth-round pick was the highest drafted player in school history and held a stat line that looked like a video game feature. He proved his worth to wear the uniform, but the first half of his very first season in professional baseball was a rude awakening. He just couldn't get anything started, and the season's struggle began to wear on him.

After that at-bat, Brian walked back to the dugout in a slow burn. He was ready to melt down and was caught up in his own world. He gave into the temptation with a few knee-jerk reactions but then he took a seat on the bench, alone. It happens a lot in the dugout. These boys are trying to become men, but maturing is never clean or simple.

The players repelled from him and stayed clear of the firing range. They dropped eye contact, pretended he wasn't there, and by golly under zero circumstances would they go over and talk to him. But as he stared off into no man's land trying to escape his own mind, he felt a tap on his leg. He looked down to hear, "O'Keefe, it's OK. You'll have more chances." Josiah looked up at Brian: "But no matter what, you just need to fight. That's all you can do."

Just like that, Brian snapped back to reality, and with a little grin and sigh of relief he said, "You're absolutely right, buddy, thank you."

There was something so simple yet so genuine about that interaction. To everyone else in the dugout, it was something they wouldn't dare try. Josiah was the only one in the dugout to face the issue head on, and without devaluing anyone or embarrassing him, Josiah made his point clear. In his own words, O'Keefe looked back on that day and said, "You always hear baseball is just a game, but you never really look at it that way. You're always chasing that next perfect swing or perfect play, rarely seeing it as just a game. Well for me, Josiah showed me what is truly important and when he did that, I couldn't help but think of everything

I take for granted on a daily basis. From that moment on I started to fight for the game more than I ever had."

There was something about Josiah in the dugout. I tried to stay out of everyone's business and let this be Josiah's fun—though he usually ran off with his friends before I even had the chance to cramp his style—but it was tough to ignore the relationships and the impact this little boy was creating.

Over the course of the season, Collin and I became close. He told me about the impact Josiah's batting practice had on him, and it was great to see his season finally improve. The days he wasn't playing we would talk about baseball, Josiah, our walk in faith, or anything else we felt was heavy on our hearts.

One night late in the season, Collin and I struck up a conversation and he started teaching me about baseball—the culture, the players, strategies, goals—and the ins and outs of the minor league system. But he told me this team was different. I didn't know what he meant and I asked him why.

He said to me that Minor League Baseball usually becomes an individual game. A player's ultimate goal is to get to the major leagues, and like any business, the way to do that is to continually earn promotions and move up the ladder. So, a team's success is greatly overshadowed by a player's individual success, and the most competition is usually within your own dugout, not against it.

It's a sad reality, but the more selfish players sometimes root for a teammate's failure—especially within their own position—but even the most team-oriented guys know their stint with a minor league affiliate is only temporary, as the main goal is to reach the big leagues.

I started to understand, but then he told me again with the same conviction that this team was different.

I got the struggle he was talking about—the long nights on a bus, the daily challenges of the game, the minor league life living on an energy bar and a cup of coffee—but I didn't get what he meant every time he said this team was different. He began to smile and told me that individual success still remained in focus, but this was the only team that had something else to play for; something more than baseball.

He said he had never seen or been in a clubhouse with a group of guys that cared so much about something other than hits or results and had really underestimated how quickly the team bought in to Josiah's request for a championship.

All of a sudden, it clicked, and I realized the impact I could never see. I guess I could see the surface-level impact Josiah made with these guys—a special handshake, a quick smile, or a moment in their day to just laugh—but I couldn't see Minor League Baseball through the eyes of a player. I didn't know what they went through or how his story hit them; but I do know Collin, Chase, Danny, and Nick all saw something extraordinary in this little boy, and the team followed suit.

23

JOSIAH'S CHAMPIONSHIP

THE PRESS CAUGHT WIND of a story about a little kid in the dugout. From the ESPN *E:60*, to the jersey, to the relationship with the team, Josiah's story spread like wildfire throughout the baseball world. The season continued on and headed toward another playoff run and Josiah did more interviews and the team kept winning. In the first week of September, the Spikes found themselves in a decisive Game Three for the New York-Penn League Championship.

Josiah made it known all year that he wanted a championship. He obsessed over the hunt for "the ring," as he kept saying, and probably annoyed them with his badgering, but now we were here! We got to travel with the team through all the playoffs, and now we were set to square off for the deciding Game Three of the NYPL Championship with the team that knocked us out the year before, the Tri-City Valley Cats.

There was a foggy haze under the lights on a cold New York September night, and I couldn't help but be nervous. The team went through their normal routine of handshakes and hugs before the game, relieving the pregame jitters, when one of the pitchers yelled over to Josiah, "How many runs you want, Jo?"

Josiah finished his handshakes and hugs and yelled back, "Thirteen!"

Shaking his head and laughing at such an outrageous number, the pitcher yelled to the dugout, "If that's what he wants, we're getting him thirteen!" The Spikes charged onto the field.

After nine innings and an 11-2 victory, the State College Spikes were NYPL Champions. The team celebrated in the clubhouse with a sparkling cider shower (instead of the usual champagne because half the team was under twenty-one) and the pitcher came up to Jo with a huge grin and an oversized bottle of cider: "Thirteen, huh?"

The season came to a close with the championship ring Josiah had his heart set on. But that summer meant more than just a championship to those kids on the team. As players were finishing up celebrating a winning season, they began hugging Pap and Josiah, thanking them for everything they had done. Dave didn't really know how to respond. To have a team of young men thanking him just seemed backwards, and as the night went on, more and more players started to thank them for being with the team.

Josiah's four best friends walked up to him and started saying their final goodbyes. Seeing the four friends parting ways for at least another off-season almost brought tears to Dave's eyes. Collin and Chase gave Josiah a big hug and told Josiah that victory was his doing. Danny was next and, like usual, challenged him to a game of Big Three next spring training. And lastly, Thompson hugged Josiah, not knowing that the little man who gave him the courage to see grace through fire would be the ring bearer in his future wedding to the woman he started dating in the magical summer of 2014.

It was a special moment, and Dave couldn't stop thanking the guys for all they had done for Josiah. But the players would not accept a thank you. Chase pulled back from the ongoing hugs and goodbyes and said to Dave, "Thank us? Pap, we need'a thank you. Without you luggin' this little guy everywhere, we would'a never'a met one of our best friends." He looked around, gesturing to the clubhouse. "This has been a big challenge fo' all o'us, and seein' your little boy is one of our favorite parts of the day."

* * *

There was something very special about the 2014 team; something that grabbed onto the players just as much as it grabbed onto Josiah and me. We couldn't be more grateful for the year Josiah never dreamed about, and I thought it just couldn't get better than this. But there was one more surprise to top off a perfect summer.

As a way of honoring the teams that win their respective championships, the St. Louis Cardinals flew the entire coaching staff into St. Louis and had an on-field presentation before the last home series of the season. JD told us about this tradition and we couldn't be happier for Ollie's first taste of the big leagues.* He agreed and deliberately said what a wonderful trip it was going to be for the whole coaching staff.

I looked at him blankly, and he told me again: "The WHOLE coaching staff is honored." Now he's almost laughing.

"What do you mean?" I said, not wanting to draw any conclusions.

"Pack a bag; you guys are going to St. Louis."

* * *

Josiah was so excited I don't think he got a wink of sleep the entire night. I woke up to get him ready for our early-morning flight, and he was already standing on his bed, waiting for me to get him dressed. We got on the plane, and I couldn't stop thanking God for how He was working in our lives. If you told me a few years ago we would be on a flight to St. Louis, I'd think you were crazy.

As we were ready to take off for St. Louis, the pilot mumbled something over the loudspeaker and the flight became real. I buckled Josiah in for takeoff and leaned back in my chair as the plane turned for the runway. I thought about what it meant to be part of such a historic organization and what it meant to be on this flight. I thought about the guys at State College and their dream to tell their parents they got "the call" to the big leagues. But I looked at our little man and saw the smile that a team fell in love with, and as the plane accelerated down the runway, I realized for that special little boy sitting next to me, this was his dream come true; this was his call to the big leagues.

* * *

When Dave and Josiah visited Busch Stadium, the story of this little boy spread throughout the Cardinals front office. Some knew about him, some heard about him, but now people finally were able to see exactly what the

---

* After managing the Spikes, Oliver Marmol was promoted to manage the Advanced A team, the Palm Beach Cardinals in 2015. Then in 2017 he made his MLB debut as the first-base coach of the St. Louis Cardinals.

State College coaching staff has been reporting. And after their visit, Josiah was Cardinal royalty.

Later that year Dave got a call from Steve Pona, a member of the St. Louis chapter of the Baseball Writers Association of America, or BBWAA, and he told him Josiah had been chosen as that year's recipient of the Harry Mitauer Good Guy Award for his efforts at the ballpark and crucial role in the Spikes' 2014 New York-Penn League Championship run. Along with Josiah, his good friend and manager, Oliver Marmol, would be receiving the award as well.

The Good Guy award was presented to Josiah and Ollie at the annual St. Louis Baseball Writers' Dinner in January of 2015. With his little clip-on bow tie and the smallest suit they could find, Josiah walked across the stage with tears in his eyes accepting his first award as a St. Louis Cardinal to another standing ovation. Ollie received his plaque and stepped to the microphone to say a couple words of gratitude and began telling a story from the 2014 championship game. He told the crowd of the routine he shared with Josiah of checking and debating the lineups during their "lunchtime" visits. The crowd laughed and he continued to explain that most days Josiah would agree and give the lineup a stamp of approval, but some days Josiah would challenge it and Ollie would have to give an explanation.

Well, until this night, no one knew that decisive Game Three of the New York-Penn League Championship game was one of the lineups he had challenged; Josiah had told his manager to put in a player who hadn't seen a live at-bat in over a week.

To the naked eye that may not seem like a big deal, but to a player facing a pitcher throwing above ninety miles per hour with off-speed pitches to keep you off-balance, without consistent at-bats, a player's timing will be seriously off. So Ollie explained this to Josiah before he left to go play cards with his friends. But something didn't sit right with Ollie. He looked at his lineup and thought about the suggestion, and before he sent the official roster to the umpires, Ollie made a last-minute switch.

The Spikes went on to win their first-ever New York-Penn league championship by a rally started in the very first inning of the game. Six runs capped off the top of the inning followed by five more to win. In the first inning, with one out, the player to start that impressive rally was the last-minute switch that resulted in two hits and another three RBIs to solidify the win.

*   *   *

I held Josiah with his Good Guy plaque resting in his lap and couldn't help but well up with tears. Players and coaches from our trip to Busch Stadium swarmed us the entire night, and the same chills that ran down my spine when stepping on the field in St. Louis had now returned while holding my little boy. People no longer saw him as an inspiring story or a charity case; they saw him as a symbol of courage, a message to fight.

The truth is, Josiah may not ever have a choice in the direction of his life, but he has always made the choice to walk in courage. The greatest lesson he ever taught these young men is that we as human beings all have a choice. In every situation, we have a choice to let our situation consume us, or to rise up, to stand, and endure. With each batting practice they watched, with each grimace of pain they saw, Josiah showed the team what it looks like to choose courage over fear and to choose love over pain.

He showed them to fight.

Collin was right; this team *was* different. They saw the light God put inside this little boy and they chose to follow it.

PART 3

CHANGE

Josiah is getting old—not growing up, or becoming the young teenager his age suggests—but growing old. The cute rosy red cheeks that once bubbled around his boyish smile have begun to wrinkle and sag like mine, as his body begins to wither and hunch with every step. The brutal reality is that Progeria is no longer the future; it is now the harsh reality of a little boy.

Although the hardest chapters of our lives have yet to be written, Part Three shows us that a life of choice is the only life that matters, and Josiah shows us that joy will forever overcome pain, courage will forever endure fear, and love will live on forever.

Time is spinning, and Part Three holds on to the only seconds we are promised—today.

24

BECOMING A FAMILY

JEN KNEW IN COLLEGE. She felt it long before her first girl-friend, but she also knew I would never accept a life outside of the teachings of the fire and brimstone that spewed out of my anger long ago. So she didn't tell me—she couldn't.

I put it together before she had to ever say anything, but I couldn't come to terms with the thought of my daughter loving another woman. I spent restless nights thinking about our family, how far we had come, and the journey we were on. But I couldn't think about my daughter. I couldn't accept it. I wouldn't. I was done with the conversation before it started.

I thought about Josiah and Daisha and the sudden change that now enveloped their lives. I was wrestling with myself, back and forth, between the love I have for my daughter and a lifestyle I couldn't understand. It's a lifestyle of sin and God will not allow sin into the Kingdom of Heaven. I just couldn't understand how anyone could rightfully choose that life without thinking of the consequences that follow. I thought about judgment. I thought about righteousness and the Kingdom of Heaven; and after everything we had been through with Josiah, my faith was certain on the Lord. The Bible is clear; homosexuality is wrong, and I couldn't accept my own daughter.

Living in silence was a familiar pain to her, but the sharp blade of judgment was not. I may have always wound our relationship tighter than a drum, but through the diagnosis and every medical hurdle we jumped over, Jen and I only worked together.

But I never asked how she was dealing with Josiah or the life she was given, and I never even asked if she wanted to talk. I was too blind to see the pain Jen was in.

It was new to us both, but Jen knew if she told me that she was gay, the love she thought we found in room 282 would be destroyed, along with everything we had worked so hard to build. So she bottled it. She chose the suffering that remained familiar, and the happiness Josiah's life brought us began to elude once again.

Love was only pain. And now Jen was told to care for a child for the rest of his short life, all while she couldn't even love herself. Her entire life, the idea of love had been a just fleeting journey that usually ended in pain. From her childhood being deprived by parents who never seemed to love anyone, to the list of relationships that left her a single mother trying to provide for a family, to bearing a child who would only be ripped from her arms in a few short years—love had forgotten her. And if love ever showed up in her life again, it had some explaining to do.

Trying to live a double life to keep everyone else happy tore her in half, and her secret became a wedge not only separating herself from our family, but a wedge separating herself from the life she deserved.

So one day, as the darkest of days continued to surround her fleeting life, she decided to tell us. With tears in her eyes and a lump in her throat, she blurted it out. She told us point-blank, and let the words ring out in silence while she waited for the jury to deliver their verdict.

Jen was finally free, but liberation never comes without opposition. Although the road she was now traveling would be rocky and tough, she could begin to heal, and the love that once died within her heart could now reenter and save the life that was once passed. She became the woman she had to be. Even though I may not ever agree with some of her choices, her walk through pain finally brought her to love.

She looked up at us after telling us she was gay, and silence fell over all of us.

Deb was actually OK with it. I was not. I became so righteous in my own walk in faith that I became blind to everything that makes up being a Christian. At the time, I believed I was right and she was wrong, so I stood firm. But what I didn't understand was the grace God had given us. I thought I was seeking justice. I thought I was righteous. But the fact that I would just give up on my own daughter because of something I don't agree with became a hypocrisy built on a lie.

I didn't understand the grace God gave to me when he brought my family together in room 282. I didn't understand the forgiveness God gave to me when he pulled on my heart during a Wednesday group meeting at Four Square Church after years of turning my back on faith. I didn't understand the love my family gave to me when they allowed me to remain in their lives after the childhood of torment and anger I gave to them. I was accepted through every flaw, and now I wouldn't accept my own daughter because I thought I saw one in her?

With tears streaming down her face, Jen knew the message of my silence. She picked her head up from the table and in one breath said into my eyes, "I'm not asking you to agree. I'm not asking you to accept it. I'm just asking you to love me."

*   *   *

Jen hung up the phone and scheduled a time and place for lunch with her newly found friend, Liz Pysher. Jen reached out to Liz regarding a family friend's medical situation, and being the kind-hearted person she is, Liz of course agreed. Liz is another country-strong woman from outside of Schuylkill Valley with a bachelor's degree in psychology from Penn State University. She's a tough woman, but as loving as they come, and when someone needs assistance, she would go to the ends of the earth to make sure they were safe.

The day came to sit down over a hot cup of coffee at the local diner, but what started as a twenty-minute interview about their mutual friend ended three hours later with something poking at their hearts. Jen was already burned by too many toxic relationships to count, and it seemed as though Liz was paddling in the same boat. So they made clear boundaries; they were friends—nothing more.

Liz started coming to the house more frequently, and honestly, I had trouble with it. A lot of it. They began hanging out every once in a while when the other just needed a break. I didn't like seeing another woman around the house, and regrettably, I barely acknowledged Liz's existence.

They were both guarded. Both were wounded from past relationships that left scars deeper than they'd like to admit, so they remained close. Liz was becoming a fixture over at the house, and nights spent at the local diner together became a delight they looked forward to for days in advance. But they were friends—nothing more.

After months of spending time with one another, caring for one another, and opening up to one another, before they knew it they were spinning deeper in love than the boundaries their friendship allowed. One Saturday afternoon, they decided to take a walk around the park to escape the world together. There's a place near town called the Valley View Park where the stream cuts through the park and the world seems to be as still as the gently trickling water. A bench sits right at the mouth of the stream, just far enough away to take a moment and absorb the beauty of the lush mountainside but close enough to eavesdrop on the whispering creek.

Jen and Liz walked through the park side by side talking about nothing. They each rambled on as long as they could until their thoughts and words no longer could avoid what their hearts were saying. They sat down on the wooden bench and pretended to absorb the breathtaking view until finally, Jen broke the silence.

"We keep saying we are just friends."

"Yes," Liz said plainly, although she knew exactly what Jen meant.

"But, I don't know—you're over at our house every day, you come over after work, and we both care so much about each other, but it's just—friends . . ."

They sat in silence.

Liz finally turned to Jen and asked point-blank, "So what are we doing here?"

Jen looked up at Liz, and they both saw the love and compassion in each that had fostered the day they met for coffee.

"Let's do this," she said, breaking into the faintest appearance of a smile. "Together."

* * *

They left the park and they were officially a couple, but they had an announcement to make that would not be as easy. I know I made it tough on them, and now more than ever, the family needed each other. We made a vow to never divide the family again, and Liz had to be accepted by every one of them—including Daisha. Of course, Deb and I already knew Liz was more than just a friend, but it didn't mean I had accepted their lifestyle. They would come over to the house, now as a couple, and it was hard. Change never came easy, but I made a promise to choose love before judgment. No matter what, I would reach for love. After all, they're family.

* * *

As Liz remained with us, Josiah was now nine years old and started to warm up to the idea of having Liz around for good. Piggyback rides and playful nightly wrestling matches made Liz and Josiah able to connect almost instantly.

But like her Pap, Daisha was a tough one to crack. She was growing like a weed, playing softball, and talking nonstop, but the shell of strength that wrapped around her was the same tough skin that wrapped around her as she stayed in room 282 with Josiah and her mom. She was a tough kid, and a few piggyback rides and a wrestling match were not enough to break into the heart of this little girl. To Daisha, her mom's past relationships ended in tears she never wanted to share.

It was hard. Not just being accepted by Daisha or myself, but life in general. As happy as Jen and Liz were, coming to terms with a child with Progeria lingered over their heads every night. How were they—or any of us—supposed to give the happiness this little boy deserved while making him comprehend having two mommies, when that had never been part of his world before? It wasn't easy, and we didn't know what to do, but all we wanted was to remain together—face everything as a family and keep pressing forward. That helped, but it didn't solve anything.

Liz did everything; she cooked for the family, she cleaned the house, she got the kids ready for school, all while working full time. It all seemed to be for nothing. Just like any two stubborn country folk from the coal region, change does not happen quickly for Daisha or me. And the more Liz tried, the further she seemed to be pushed away. It was as if no matter how many meals she put into Tupperware for my late-night snack or how many yellow Tastycakes she put into Daisha's lunch, she would forever be an outsider.

But everything she didn't notice, Daisha and I did.

I've never been a man of many words, but I started intentionally inviting Liz to family dinners. They may not have had the most ravishing conversations or the most heartfelt exchanges, but I began to show her that she was welcomed, and it was the start she deserved.

Daisha, on the other hand, loves her baby brother more than her own life, so the more she saw Liz take care of Josiah, the more Daisha began warming up to her. I knew if Josiah told Liz that he loved her, Daisha would too.

The kids were at the age where sleeping alone made their rooms alive and the darkness became an eerie creepiness that could only be fixed by their mom. Jen would switch off sleeping next to Josiah's bed, then move to Daisha's room. It was their nightly routine, and a tax every mother wishes to have back once their kids grow.

As Liz grew into the family, Liz would sleep next to Josiah's bed at night while Jen would sleep with Daisha. As much as Liz loved being with Josiah, she knew the only reason she remained in Josiah's room was that Daisha only wanted her mommy there— and that meant not Liz.

Daisha still only wanted her mommy. It wasn't about having two mommies or even trying to understand what that meant, but every person who had come into their lives had left, and all she saw were the broken pieces of her mom that she couldn't pick up. So, like any little girl who had to watch her mommy cry when yet another spouse walked out on her family, Daisha liked Liz a lot, but she stayed on guard.

Liz continued to love the family as her own, and our conversations became easier. After my long hours at the EMT station, we would share a cup of coffee and talk about our days. It even developed to where I would call Liz for a referral when the ambulance had to transport a patient with psychiatric needs—Liz's career field. It was small, but it was the only way I knew how to show affection. Soon after, Daisha let down her guard and drew closer to Liz because of their love of animals. Walks in the park became a routine for Liz and Daisha, and their relationship grew. We were becoming a family.

Josiah found a new love for cooking and baking, so every night when Liz started dinner, a new sous-chef stood on the stool and helped her as much as he could. His now world-famous cookies—chocolate chip with extra chocolate chips—were prepared and baked by the one and only "Chef Bubby Flay."

Liz and Josiah would cook and play in the kitchen until there wasn't a chocolate chip to bake, and one day Liz even sewed Josiah his very own chef's apron—and he wouldn't take it off.

One night, Liz was getting Josiah's favorite Spider-Man pajamas on him, and as she left to prepare his toothbrush before she tucked him into bed and went to Daisha's room, a faint call from Josiah drew her back.

"Liz," Josiah said in his distinctive little crackling voice.

"Yeah, Bubby?" Liz said, running back into the room, thinking Josiah needed something.

Josiah pulled his blanket over his chest with a big smile on his face. Liz thought she must have forgotten to tuck him in and he was about to tease her to no end about it. But as she walked toward his bed looking for what she could have missed, Josiah rolled on his side and in the most innocent little voice he said, "I love ya, Liz."

In the most casual tone, Josiah finally gave Liz the piece of their family she had been longing for. She broke down, and tears instantly streamed down her face. She leaned over the bed of a boy she loved so much and gave him a kiss on his forehead.

"I love you too, Bubby."

25

2015 SPIKES

IT WAS JUNE OF 2015, and we pulled up to the park on our first day of the season with a stomach full of pregame butter-flies. We walked through the same corridor with the same smell of damp laundry and heated dryer sheets as we prepared for a whole new team and whole new experience.

I didn't think we would ever be able to top 2014, nor were we trying to. The team, Ollie, the four buddies—Chase, Danny, Collin, and Nick—and the championship will never be replaced, but as 2015 unfolded, we were given another new adventure on a journey we never dreamed about.

This year was different than the last, and after a success-ful 2014 campaign, our good friend and manager Ollie had been promoted to the Advanced-A affiliate, the Palm Beach Cardinals, and our team sponsor and general manager, JD, accepted a job in a different MiLB organization. A new wave of players poured into State College, and just like that, we once again found ourselves in unfamiliar territory.

We didn't know what to expect, but we kept walking toward the distant sign of our favorite clubhouse. Josiah was beyond excited to see the team, but I began to worry whether the new ownership and new coaching staff would allow us to remain with the team. But as soon as we reached the locker room doors, my nerves turned to excitement as an older gentleman with a gray mustache and a Cuban flare that I couldn't help but enjoy stopped us in his official State College Spikes gear, the tags freshly snapped off.

"You must be Dave and Josiah!" he said with his thick mus-tache bending into a wide smile. "I'm Johnny Rodriguez, the Spikes' manager, but call me J-Rod."

His smile lit up Josiah's face, and just like that, with a big hug from the little man, our season took off.

*   *   *

Like usual, the moment Dave and Josiah stepped into the clubhouse the team overwhelmed them with a warm reception. The players still gathered around the protective shell after every batting practice to help cheer on Josiah's world-famous "BP and Run," and Josiah was still the extra coach in the dugout giving the team a much-needed second perspective.

The guys this year made their own baseball game in the clubhouse just for Josiah. Mike Pritchard, the slap-hitting left fielder from Nebraska with his deep, ear-shattering voice that still rattles from Lincoln to State College, came in from batting practice and told everyone to move the couches. The team hustled around flipping couches into walls and throwing pillows down as bases. By the time the final player changed his cleats and entered the clubhouse-now-baseball-diamond, Josiah was holding his plastic bat, ready for the pitch. They would play a full game equipped with ghost runners and an official score, but the days they felt they needed a change, they built bigger and played home run derby.

This would go on every day before a game. Like children make forts, the ball players built a field, and no matter what age these guys claimed to be, they all became kids once again.

It had been like this the entire season, and Josiah once again had the hearts and minds of a whole stadium. The story of how a little boy and his grandfather helped propel the 2014 club to their first championship and how adored they were within the confines of Medlar Field spread throughout the New York-Penn League. The buzz of this little boy turned into a folktale around the park, and the fans couldn't get enough. It was no longer popularity, but a celebration.

As Josiah was revved and called by the PA announcer for the ceremonial first pitch, the fans once again cheered to a standing ovation, and J-Rod couldn't help but be taken aback by this little boy.

Raised in Cuba and defecting for a better life, J-Rod joked with his players about being educated by the University of Cuba and reminded his players how easy they have it and how blessed they truly are. Beneath his jokes and exaggerated humor was an undertone of seriousness and a devoted understanding about what it means to be wearing a Cardinal uniform. But what he tried to teach the young men sometimes fell short. The privileges given to most of the young ball players were never gratified nor appreciated, and their tireless pursuit of the big leagues became a meaningless dream.

It was a tough balance, usually only appreciated by a person who had seen the horrors and challenges of life, like one from Cuba—or one with Progeria.

* * *

This was all very new to us. Players walking by calling me "Pap," a nickname I only thought Josiah knew; Josiah's locker set up with a second alternate jersey to add to his collection; and introductions almost unnecessary as the new group of players knew exactly who Josiah was. The dynamic had completely changed. We were no longer the rookies hanging out with the team. We were now the veterans of the park, and players treated us just like any other personnel on the team. I spent a lot of time in J-Rod's office before games talking a little baseball, but mostly talking about our Christian walk. Those times sharing the Bible and our experiences were very special to me, and I will be always grateful for those special moments.

The dynamic at home had changed as well. I may not have been the greatest father, or the most supportive of my daughter, but now I saw a relationship between Liz and Jen that I never experienced in my life. They comfort each other and push each other to be better people. Liz shows her the love and companionship that she deserves. Liz has brought out the best parts of my daughter that I never thought I'd see again, and I love them both dearly. Though they each gained a partner, in the process, I gained two daughters. But above all else, Jen was happy, and I think when she looked in the mirror, she saw a mother for the very first time.

Liz and Jen continued to take care of each other and give each other the love they deserve, but they've also taken on new roles at home. My wife started to recover from sickness and surgery, but she could no longer take care of herself and needed full-time care. Before I could even think about limiting our baseball trips, Jen and Liz stepped in to take care of Deb around the clock. Jen knew how much baseball means to Josiah—but also to me—and she was determined to let her family experience life. I guess you can say Jen and Liz really hit a home run for us, because without them stepping to the plate, our baseball trips would be over, and by now it would just be a distant memory.

Our roles together had changed. No longer were we bickering or arguing trying to get away from each other, but rather we started to empower one another by giving the respect and devotion we so often overlooked.

Change had made us see our family in a new light.

Change forced us into experiences we never wanted to have, but it had given us new perspectives we never thought we would find. And throughout our lives together, change has allowed us to see the magnitude of each waking minute we have in this gift of life.

As Josiah began to grow up, our lives began to slow down. For a while, we stopped living in fear of the next day and stopped dwelling on things we couldn't control. As close as we were becoming, in my personal battles, I blocked out my past like a thick black Sharpie covering the sentences I wished to mask. My eyes may not be able to read what's beneath, but my heart knows every word. I was trying to move on without healing, making my wounds deepen and bleed until they drained every ounce of life from my body.

But for now, we had found ways to focus on the gift of Josiah, and it once again became a good life. The days together were filled with love, and the nights at a baseball field watching the sun skip across the sky were filled with joy. We no longer measured our days by minutes, but by moments.

*   *   *

Every Sunday during the season, a man dressed in a beige button-down collared shirt with a baseball icon pressed onto his shirt pocket walks into the clubhouse and raises his Bible announcing that Chapel would take place fifteen minutes before batting practice. It's called Baseball Chapel, and for the guys on the team, it's an opportunity to attend a church sermon if they'd like to hear a short Bible study before heading to the field.

We would sit in the pew—well, the unused locker room—and listen to the chaplain speak over the muffled disco club music thumping throughout the park. The crack of the bats mixed with the organized chaos of the opposing team's batting practice beneath the music began to drown out the message we sat down to hear. One particular message started to fade into the noise behind the chaplain, and he looked over to Josiah and asked if he would like to say a couple of words.

Never being afraid of the spotlight, Josiah hopped up onto his lap and just began talking. I don't know where it came from. I don't know how he knew what to say, but the moment he started talking, the clubhouse went silent, and their batting practice seemed to fade beneath the soft voice of a little boy.

He spoke about life, fulfillment, the joy in what you do, and the will to never ever stop fighting. His words resonated in their hearts, and at the end of Josiah's sermon every player went over to give him a hug. I shook the chaplain's hand to thank him, but he grabbed my arm and said, "No, thank you for this little boy. It would be foolish of me to try and preach about life when this little boy knows more about it than any one of us sitting here."

He was right.

The young men listened to the message they heard from this little boy and were inspired to do the same in every aspect of their own lives. For the past few years his influence resonated throughout the State College Spikes, and now the Spikes had decided to commemorate his impact by creating the Josiah Viera Award.

When we were told the Spikes were creating an award given to one player on the Spikes team that represented Josiah's courage to persevere we couldn't have been more honored. And if the award wasn't special enough already, they asked Josiah to handpick each year's recipient. In a meeting with GM Scott Walker, I was somewhat shocked when Scott said, "Dave, no one in this room knows the team better than Josiah. He's the only one that can give this award."

So, when asked who would be the 2015 recipient of the Josiah Viera Award, without hesitation, Josiah said, "Jose."

"Jose?"

"Yes, Jose."

* * *

Two outs, a runner on first and one on second, bottom of the ninth, and the game was all tied up at one. The stage was set, and the State College Spikes catcher, Jose Godoy, stepped to the plate. Like most of the Spikes, Jose got off to a slow start, but a good at-bat here could be just the spark the team needed.

Ball four.

The place went crazy. Now, the bottom of the ninth became the backyard dream of any young boy—bases loaded, two outs, game tied, winning run on third—and the Spikes' hottest hitter, Casey Grayson, dug into the box. Unlike the rest of the team, Casey started the season red hot and was still hitting over .350.

The opposing team's pitching coach ran out to the mound to talk strategy with his young pitcher, but it was no use. Casey was locked in. He stepped into the box and rifled a line drive into center field, and the Spikes won the game—or so they thought.

The team mobbed Casey after a well-deserved walk-off single, and the crowd stood to their feet. Just the win they needed to get back into the playoff hunt. While the team celebrated on the field, the umpires, who had left the playing field, came back onto the field. What happened next changed the entire Spikes season.

The opposing team protested the single, and as it turned out, the runner on first base, Jose, never touched second. This violation meant Jose was actually the third out, and the run didn't score.

The team couldn't believe it. All Jose needed to do was touch the base and the game was over, but the mental error cost them the victory, and the game continued.

The ballpark was empty—so empty that workers were cleaning the stadium as the game crawled forward, and the game that seemed to never end remained deadlocked at one. The extra inning affair turned the clock well past midnight and deep into the fourteenth inning, the wrong end of a rally woke up the opposing team's bats, and the Spikes suffered one of the most disheartening losses of the season.

The clubhouse fell into a silence louder than any celebration that had occurred here only a few hours ago. The post-game spread was already cold, sitting there since the eighth inning, which felt like light-years ago, and the loss seemed to linger around each player. Jose could barely lift his head from his locker, and the team was too drained to even say a word. What started as a spark the struggling team needed turned into a bitter affair that pushed the season further into the distance.

*   *   *

With a team of four all-stars and more promotions than I can count, when Josiah named their .230 hitting catcher, Jose Godoy, for the Josiah Viera Award, he raised a lot of eyebrows.

People wanted to know, why Jose? What made Jose so special that Josiah would make the first-ever Josiah Viera Award go to a player who slid under the radar for the entire year other than a blunder that cost the team a win? And in his soft squeaky voice, Josiah said, "Because after that night [of the base-running mistake], Jose threw out several base runners in a row and only made one error the entire season."

Not knowing how Josiah knew or even understood those stats, I was taken aback. But before I could give him approval he continued: "He was our best defensive catcher this season, but Pappy—" he said, tilting his cap back, looking directly into my eyes, "he never gave up."

26

THE FUTURE

JOSIAH TURNED TWELVE.

The reality of rapid aging was no longer anticipated; it had arrived. The regular checkups with Dr. Walsh were now conversations about keeping his blood pressure stable and his heart strong—almost foreshadowing the types of conversations I will be having in just a few years with my own physician. Josiah was growing old and with each breath he took, we feared for the next.

But like usual, Dr. Walsh found ways to adjust and found solutions to handle every problem that came our way. We worked to give him sustainability; more sleep, less running around—and Josiah's least favorite—less batting practice when the weather was too hot. But no matter how much we adjusted and planned our days, the future crept in from its far, distant place in our minds, and now it was the only reality that we could see.

This was Josiah's second year receiving his very own baseball card, but it was his first year attending the State College Spikes meet-and-greet as part of the team. Josiah loves every second he's with the team, but this one was special. Having his very own seat at the table of players, signing autographs, and getting to be up close and personal with all the fans made him feel like he was a major leaguer. Even today, I pray that feeling never leaves him.

Everyone entered the park and received a brand-new pack of State College Spikes baseball cards. They walked down the line of players and received an autograph by each one—including Josiah. Just like the Children's Miracle Network convention, people couldn't wait to get their Josiah Viera baseball card officially signed by Josiah himself, and his corner of the autograph line became swamped with fans.

He signed as much as he could, but soon his hand slowed down. Like everything he does, he tried to simply manage the pain so he could continue, but his body was starting to give out. The pen began jumping from his hand, and his once-steady "JOSIAH #10" autograph became a chopped, scratchy version that looked just as painful as it felt. He didn't understand what was happening to his body.

"Let's head back, Bubby," I said, trying to keep him as positive as possible.

"No," Josiah answered, struggling to sign his name.

His hand could now barely grip the pen. He was in more pain than we'd ever know, but he would never say anything. He loved every minute of being with the fans and was not about to leave. Finally, he tried to sign another card, but the pen popped out of his fingers, and his hand began shaking.

"OK. Pappy, I'm done."

I could see his eyes start to get puffy. He didn't know what was happening to his body or why holding a pen was almost unattainable. All he remembered was the strength he once had—and the life he once lived.

"It's OK, Bubby," I said, trying not to well up with tears. "I think it's time to head back."

I tried to comfort him, but how could I comfort a child fighting a disease that made us see death before it comes? How could I tell my child it's OK when he knew the strength he once had was slowly draining while his pain was rising?

All I could do was watch as he began to see a narrative he never wished to have.

I guess by now I should have expected these things or at least be ready for them. But it's hard for me to anticipate his weakest moments when he gives us so much strength. The way he strengthens my mind but softens my heart, the way he shows me joy instead of loss, and the way he brings my family together with a flash of his smile; every day I'm around Josiah my life is that much better. He's my little man and my best friend.

I picked Josiah up and he latched around my neck. We headed back to the locker room. As we were leaving the autograph table the players kept him positive.

"See you in the dugout, Jo," they'd yell. And the folks who got Josiah's autograph thanked him so much that we could barely get a word in. But as we were walking away, I glanced into the eyes of those fans around the table realizing the fans just got a first-hand look at the harsh reality of an unforgiving disease. I saw some with tears and others with eyes of compassion. Many were just glad they had the opportunity to see Josiah that day and just say hello. But they all saw a young boy struggle to hold a pen. They saw a frail hand shake with pain, as he could no longer carry on. They saw the cold introduction of a story no child should tell.

It's taken us a while to just enjoy the day and not worry about the future, but in moments like this, it hits me that Josiah is now twelve years old. It's something I hated to think about and is something I still struggle with today. No matter how much we tried to forget, or how tightly we hold onto the moments we're given, the truth is, Josiah's time is limited.

27

BOBBLEHEAD NIGHT

THE 2015 SEASON CAME to a close, and it was now late autumn back in Hegins, Pennsylvania. The crisp autumn air replaced the warm summer nights, and I revolved around the same fifteen channels hopelessly dreaming a new channel would appear to fill the void of our nightly summer baseball games. But the only Cardinal red we could see was slowly diluting the thick green forest over the mountainside.

Admittedly, it was a heartbreaking time for die-hards around the country and a pity party only sympathized by sports fans alike. But just as our baseball season was blanketed over by winter's warning, the phone rang, and our good friends at Medlar Field had exciting news—and next summer couldn't get here soon enough.

"Jen." I called her as soon as I hung up the phone with the GM, Scott Walker. "You're not gonna believe this. They're having Josiah Viera Night at the park, and Josiah is getting his very own bobblehead!"

"Wow! That's going to be such a special night." Her mouth could barely keep up with her words. "This is . . . this is incredible."

"They want to keep it a surprise, though. Once they get the final bobblehead design, then we tell him."

"That's a good idea. Dad, he's gonna love this."

"Yeah," I said with a changing sense of sadness. "He will. I just hope he sees it."

Jen caught my concern.

"Dad, he's going to see this," she said firmly.

"You're right, but I—"

"Dad. He's going to have this day."

She was right, but it was still hard for me to think about the future. Whether it was planning five years down the road or planning next week's dinner, it frightened me and became that same black hole I've tried to hide from my entire life. I knew my little boy was the strongest person I've ever met, but the harsh reality that Josiah will one day not be able to see the impact that he's made weakens me, and I fall.

But since the day we put aside our differences, Jen continues to give me the strength I need and the love this family needs even more. Ever since she and Liz entered our lives as a couple, they have been the rocks we need and the mothers their children deserve.

* * *

That day was inherently different than anything we had ever experienced on the baseball field. From the television interviews, radio broadcasts, and film crews capturing our every step, and finding out ESPN was there to film their second *E:60* on Josiah; it was quite the whirlwind. Even the weeks leading up to this day, Josiah was the spotlight of a mini promotional tour, and he loved it.

It was so special to see Josiah not just being part of the team or being honored, but getting the spotlight on the field. I still remember when we let the cat out of the bag and I was able to tell him the Spikes were having Josiah Viera Day at the park. We showed him the design of the bobblehead the first thousand fans would receive, and he was so excited that he kept yelling, "That's me, Pappy, that's me!"

He deserved this day, and it was finally here.

To be completely honest, it's hard to describe that night. It's hard to explain the feeling of excitement bouncing off the clubhouse walls as Josiah put on his favorite Spikes uniform. It's difficult to replay the waterfall of emotion flowing throughout the stands when Josiah was getting ready to be called from the dugout. And it's impossible to feel that certain electricity that buzzed through Medlar Field. It was as if everyone knew something special was going on, but no one could put their finger on it.

Finally, PA announcer called Josiah out to the mount for his big moment and cheers echoed throughout the stadium. Through a line of paparazzi, he stood in front of the mound, tipping his cap to the crowd, and the fans rose to their feet. As if we were back in Florida at the CMN convention, the fans would not sit down. Josiah stood there for a few extra seconds, allowing the applause to simmer down. He wound up and delivered a strike—again; it's a strike to us—to his teammate, Danny Hudzina.

As the roars echoed throughout the stadium, I looked up to find our family. There they were. Standing on the balcony of the million-dollar view as their teary eyes undoubtedly matched the crowd's. Josiah looked for his mommies and our family, and he jumped and smiled, waving to each and every one. Daisha, Jen, and Liz stood outside the box, waving back at Josiah and sharing a conversation they will only know.

He told ESPN one of the best parts of the day was having his entire family watching him play baseball with his friends. Josiah's heart will never stop growing, and the love for his family is something we all feel each and every day.

And then we saw the rest of our family.

There was Stephanie Wesner from Children's Two with tears in her eyes, soaking in a moment no one ever believed to be possible. Bonnie Tharp and our friends from the Children's Miracle Network, cheering next to our family, smiling from ear to ear. And in the corner of my eye, I looked up and saw Dr. Walsh.

This day belonged to her.

From everything she put herself through to protect my family—the extra shifts in the PICU, the nights she held our family when we couldn't hold ourselves, and the tears she shed the night before she knew we had to turn off his ventilator—she deserved this.

She stood there with her husband and daughter, cheering and crying and cheering some more, as if her child were the one throwing out the first pitch. My eyes filled with tears. I couldn't help but smile knowing this night was as much as hers as it was Josiah's. *That's our family in that booth,* I told myself, and I thanked God for the million-dollar view he had given to all of us in Josiah.

* * *

ESPN's Ben Houser remained in the dugout filming the follow-up *E:60* documentary and captured the moments with the team. On that particular night, past MLB All-Star St. Louis Cardinal Hall of Fame inductee Willie McGee Jr., was in town along with past MLB veteran Ryan Ludwick, who was standing next to me as we leaned over the guardrail, sharing the game together.

It really didn't hit me until Ben called me over, flipping his camera around to show me a few still shots of our time in the dugout. I saw the joy on my little boy's face, but I saw it recipro-cated on everyone around him.

"This is amazing," Ben said, dropping his camera to his hip and looking around the dugout. "I don't know of anywhere in baseball where a twelve-year-old boy and his grandfather are in the dugout for games. This is just simply amazing."

He was right. Perhaps I didn't realize the magnitude of where we were.

Standing next to all-time St. Louis greats as they watched from the sidelines of a day dedicated to my grandson does not happen every day. This *was* amazing. This was simply amazing.

The game got underway, and I took my spot at the end of the dugout—just right of the hallway, just left of the bench. From all the games I've posted up against this wall to watch Medlar Field illuminate the diamond while the sky turned black, I wouldn't be surprised if there was a permanent indentation where my hip rested against the pine.

I looked out onto the field trying to absorb the magic of the night while the glow of the stadium lights made the players be-neath them become more like idols rather than players. The fans, the stadium, and the evening spent watching their favorite home-town team brought a smile to everyone's face, but as a firm gust of wind swirled around the park, the left field BBQ pit pulled at the fans in more ways than the baseball game ever could.

I looked out onto the field trying to absorb the magic of the night. The glow of the stadium lights beamed down on the field making the players beneath look more like idols rather than baseball players. I saw the crowd and every young fan dreaming to feel the stadium lights the way these young men did right now. Being adored, cheered, and followed by one of the most dedicated fan bases in all of the sports is a boyhood dream that will forever be romanticized but lived by only a few.

I have nothing but gratitude toward the St. Louis Cardinals organization, and everyone we have had the pleasure of meeting along the way. It was those people who made this night so special. But as the night slowly burn down to its wick, a sadness came over me.

I felt guilty feeling so sad after a night of such joy, but it began to sink in. The days spent with the team and nights spent amongst the greatest game in the world has made our lives fuller than we ever imagined, but the truth is, we no longer question *if* Josiah's nights at the park would come to an end—but *when*.

28

HEAVEN'S GATES

W E NEVER LOST SIGHT that the quality of life is the only life that matters, but now the quantity of Josiah's is shortening, and I just couldn't let myself have the same happiness we once had at the ballpark. Happiness always traveled beside us like the friend we looked forward to seeing, but now it seemed as though Emptiness arrived at my doorstep soon after. After the bobblehead night, Josiah was with his mom and couldn't make the Saturday matchup at Medlar Field, so we told J-Rod we would see them the next day. But for some reason, I wanted to be at the park.

I needed to experience a game alone and prove to myself that I could do it, that I could be here alone and everything would just remain the same.

Yes, this will be fun, I kept saying to try and make myself believe that Happiness would make the trip with me. I would get a seat, and for the first time, *I'll get to relax and enjoy a baseball game from the comfort of the stands.* I knew this was not going to be the relaxing night at the ball field I was hopelessly telling myself it would. But I knew I had to do it. So I drove to the stadium and got a ticket.

I can't remember much of the game, but I was never there for baseball. No comforting self-talks to pretend I was here on vacation, no pregame butterflies. Just a lead balloon in my stomach knowing this was not the glorious homecoming I pretended it was.

I walked around the concourse, looking at the stadium in the way I used to—as a fan.

People passed by me, and I passed by them. The game had already started, but I hadn't noticed. My mind was in a fog. I sat down in my seat, and although the curved plastic seating wrapped around my backside to form the perfect fit, it would never replace the cold comfort of the hard, wooden bench in the dugout. I kept asking myself if I could do this, if I could enjoy baseball on my own, or if this too would also become just a memory we once held.

And I just couldn't.

I sat and stared at a game I once felt before, and now the field was dull. The night sky I used to watch God paint before fading to black was now just gray, and the only thing gripping my attention on the diamond was the music being played between innings. This wasn't the same, it wouldn't ever be the same, and as if Emptiness took the ticket from my hand, my world was now fuzzy on its ends.

Happiness didn't just stand me up tonight. Slowly it was becoming more distant and more elusive as Josiah was growing older. And tonight, Happiness only left me its void of a relationship that Emptiness was surely filling.

It was the third inning, and I couldn't help but think about what Josiah would be saying to the team on the bench. Josiah would go through all of his handshakes before the game, throw out the first pitch, and then watch the game like a hawk until the bottom of this inning, and then we would start our routine.

A few months prior, our good friend and "Voice of the Spikes," Joe Putnam, along with fellow announcer Steve Jones, told us to come up to the broadcast booth whenever we'd like. Their warm smiles and large personalities coupled with two of the most recognizable voices in the central Pennsylvania region made the initial invitation an offer I couldn't refuse. But this was Josiah's team, and taking him from the dugout was nearly impossible. I thanked Joe and Steve but told them I wasn't sure if Josiah would ever leave the field so we might need to pass. He understood but said the offer would always be on the table.

But one game when Josiah was craving some cheese fries, selfishly, I tempted him.

"Hey, Bubby, why don't we make a cheese fry run and go up to say hi to our friend Joe in the booth?"

Maybe it was a little unfair because enticing Josiah with cheese fries is like tempting a shark with blood, but Josiah thought it was a fair deal, and we headed up to the booth.

Joe and Steve greeted us, and we were instantly taken aback by the breathtaking view of the broadcast booth. The stadium always looked like home to us, but now it looked like a work of art. Everything seemed so quaint and pristine that I couldn't help but look at the stadium like an artist looks at a masterpiece. I think Josiah was more intrigued by the radio broadcast and the headsets that followed, but nonetheless, it was shaping up to be a trip well worth the elevator ride.

Between innings, Joe explained the show and how the online streaming works, but we were floored by just being able to watch the Voice of the Spikes go to work. Then, after an inning passed by, Joe turned to Josiah and with a big smile said, "So, do you want to go on air?"

Before he could finish his question, Josiah jumped up on the seat and reached for the headphones he'd been eyeing all game. Joe went over some of the questions and told Josiah the ins and outs of a broadcast, but Josiah is quite the ham on camera, and a radio show was a walk in the park for him.

The broadcast came back from commercial, and in one breath it was like the Voice of the Spikes unhitched his horse from its buggy: "WEL-come-back-everyone-to-the SIXTH inning of our-Saturday-night-matchup between-the-visiting Williamsport Crosscutters and YOUR Staaate College Spikes!" Before the inning even started he excited the airwaves with the twang and elegance only the Voice of the Spikes could deliver.

He welcomed Josiah as his new guest and then coined a phrase that soon became a household name throughout central Pennsylvania: "I'm here with our special guest and Spikes bench coach Josiah Viera, here with the newest addition of . . . Action Innings."

Without a hitch, Josiah introduced himself the only way he knows how: talking baseball. The sweetness of Josiah's rough and squeaky voice paired with the music of Joe's soothing sound created such a beautiful conversation that you just couldn't help but listen. They talked stats, strategy, upcoming opponents, players on the team, and anything else that came to either of their minds just like their very own episode of *Baseball Tonight*. But as the eighth inning rolled around and the Spikes needed a late-inning rally to win, Josiah said it was time to head back to the dugout.

We thanked Joe and Steve and they thanked us.

"I can't believe how well that went," I said, half-joking to Joe.

"He's a pro!" Joe said, looking at Josiah. "That was the most fun we've had in the booth for a long time, buddy." Without hesitation Steve agreed and asked, "How 'bout some more Action Innings tomorrow?"

Josiah looked at me for approval.

"Well, yeah. If that's OK with you, Bubby?"

"Yeah! Action Innings, tomorrow night, we'll be here."

So the next night—and every night after that—we would continue our routine of cheese fries then Action Innings. They would chat away for two innings filled with stories from the clubhouse, stats from the game, and analysis from the little voice of Josiah Viera and the narrating music of Joe's. I would just sit back and listen to the magic happen.

But after a few days of our routine, Joe told us something very humbling. He said after the past few home stands, the listeners of the broadcast had almost doubled, and the Spikes media was now overflowing with messages and posts about how much they loved hearing Josiah on the radio.

Even the producer of the broadcast had told us how great it was to hear that little voice come over the radio. He was the guy who sits back at the radio station, spinning dials, pushing buttons, and making sure the broadcast runs as smoothly as possible. He told us that most nights as the middle innings of the games dragged on, he started counting down the minutes until he could hear Joe Putnam announce the "Action Innings with Josiah Viera." And each night, when he heard that tiny voice come over the radio, the once-dull night of spinning dials and sitting in darkness became lifted, and he got to have the brightest three innings of his day.

When the Action Innings gained popularity, I began to think about how happy all the people listening to our little boy on the air were. I'd always smile and slightly laugh because for the people listening for three innings, that was only a glimpse of how happy that little boy makes us. His smile, his voice, his laugh, his jokes, even his singing voice when One Direction comes on Daisha's iPod is something that is just as much a part of our family as it is his own, and I don't know what we'll do when those moments are taken from us.

*   *   *

Maybe it was just out of habit, but it was now the fourth inning at my game alone, and I stood up as if it were our routine of cheese fries and Action Innings. I rode the elevator up to the media level. I thought maybe a change in scenery would let me see the game of baseball as I did for the past three years. I walked to the same broadcast booth Josiah and I had sat in many times before, and I lightly knocked on the door between innings, not knowing if I could even be here without Josiah. Steve Jones was away and Joe was doing the Spikes broadcast himself that evening.

"I'm sorry to bother you, Joe, the little man couldn't make it tonight, and I just wanted—" my voice faded, and Joe picked up on my uneasy tone. "I just wanted to see a baseball game."

I took a long breath then opened my mouth to try and explain to Joe that I was scared, I was weak, and I just didn't know what to do, but all that came out was, "Is it OK if I sit here a while?"

"Dave," he looked at me with a softening smile like the one my sister used to comfort me with when we were kids hiding from our father. "You are always welcome here; have a seat."

I guess it's just the way men talk (or don't talk, I should say), but for some reason, I felt like we both understood. I sat down, and a small smile came to my face. Not because I was happy or enjoying the game, but because at my weakest moment I was once again welcomed to a family I needed.

I sat and watched the game from the same broadcast booth and realized that although I was seeing the game from the same view I had been, the game would never be the same. This game will forever remain Josiah's, and as I took a seat next to Joe, I was introduced to a game—and a life—I had never seen before.

*   *   *

Ever since our daily visits to Joe in the broadcast booth, we had become close. He became someone I could trust, and sometimes before games Joe and I would talk like old friends. The park may never be the same, but with friends like Joe, Steve, and the people at the stadium, our family knows that we are never alone.

As our friendship started to grow, our conversations would develop into more than just baseball. We'd talk about Josiah, the family, our hopes, our fears, and started to talk about what the future held, and I blurted out, "Joe, Josiah is getting older and I know at some point this is all going to come to an end. These games—these nights, all just . . . gone. Just a memory. A moment in time."

His eyes began to tear.

We shared our thoughts and talked about Josiah's love for the game of baseball but stopped short of considering again the thought of Josiah not being there. I appreciated Joe taking the time from a busy pregame schedule to sit and talk and for allowing me to pour out my heart.

* * *

Soon after my sobering conversations with Joe, I was driving the kids home from school, and I could hear Daisha whispering, "Tell him, tell him," gesturing toward Josiah to tell me something.

I looked at Josiah through the rearview mirror, staring down at the buckle of his car seat, seeming a bit bashful. Daisha kept egging him on so I told him as gently as I could, "It's OK, Josiah, you can tell me anything."

"I had a dream."

"About what?"

He paused, still staring at the buckle of his car seat.

"Tell him!" Daisha yelled, trying to pressure him into talking.

"I was in a church," Josiah began. "A big church with big windows and the light shining in the windows was really bright. And the inside of the church was a baseball field, and I was on second base. I started running the bases, and when I was running to home plate—I fell."

He paused again and looked directly at me through the rear-view mirror.

My back straightened. "What happened next?" I said softly.

"Then I slid into two big wooden doors as big as the wall. I slid into the doors, and a man opened it," he began as my knuckled clenched the steering wheel. "He just looked at me and then smiled and closed the big door. And then I woke up."

I almost pulled the car over. I'm not much on believing in dreams, but this one was a glaring message that we couldn't dismiss.

"Bubby, what did he look like?"

"He looked like a normal man. Just normal."

Taking everything in my power not to rebuttal, *Like a carpenter?* I bit my tongue and tried to wrap my head around what he meant.

"He didn't say anything?" I said to Josiah.

"No. But he smiled really big. He just smiled."

I sat there in silence.

He's not ready for him yet.

I kept saying that over and over again in my head with a strange sense of comfort passing over me. My heart pounded as I thought back to the conversation I had with Joe, and my un-grateful relationship with Emptiness, and I thought back to when Josiah was in the coma.

That little boy in his car seat may never know the miracle that came through his body, but I sure do.

I still remember looking at him, thinking that this was it, this will be the last breath he'll ever take, and I remember his eyes opening up and pinching my nose after the ventilator was turned off. I remember his miracle because I see it every day.

His miracle was not finished. Josiah is not done. Josiah is most definitely not done, and like a direct reminder from God, I hear the nurse's sweet voice from the PICU hallway: "God's not done with him yet."

29

ACCEPTANCE

BASEBALL STARTED AS JOSIAH'S adventure—his passion, his opportunity, his fun—and I just wanted to be behind the scenes making sure he was enjoying every minute of it. But as I watched our little man have the time of his life and meeting more friends than any twelve-year-old boy could ask for, I fell in love with the game of baseball for how it loved Josiah.

I never intended for Josiah's love of baseball to become mine, but it has. And now, I have become so much a part of this adventure that it actually hurts to have to abruptly leave the game at the end of each season. To be accepted as part of this baseball family to the point that this year almost everyone addresses me as "Pap," is beyond what I could have ever imagined. I have the honor of calling countless professional players, owners, and coaches my friends, and at the age of sixty-two, I feel like somehow I've just begun.

But above all, baseball has made our Bubby the happiest twelve-year-old boy in the world, and for that, I will forever love this game.

What I cherish more than the sport are the hidden lessons baseball reveals. From the strategy to the simplicity, the desire to the passion, the team to all the people we met along the way, baseball will always have a place in my heart. This is coming from a man who's never played, coached, or even been exposed to the game until much later in life. In that regard, I am undoubtedly spoiled, having been taught the game strictly by professional managers and coaches in a St. Louis Cardinals dugout. But to these kids, baseball, for the most part, has been a constant in their lives. Most grew up dreaming of becoming professional baseball players, and their dreams were finally a reality.

Along the way, the success, the struggles, the winning streaks, and the losing streaks all have been molding these young men throughout their adolescent years. I don't ever wish hardship and pain on anyone, but if baseball can provide a small glimpse of dealing with doubt, vulnerability, insecurity, and ego, their tears from this game are worth their weight in gold.

And I think that's why Josiah loves Minor League Baseball. He knows the game and knows the end goal for these kids. He knows their struggles and feels their pain. But most importantly, he knows he can show them how to overcome.

Players look at Josiah, and they see a fighter.

They see what he's been through and understand if Josiah can keep pushing through—so can they. Because the truth is, Josiah may not have chosen the life he was given, but he chooses the life he lives. Josiah was hurled into pain before he ever knew joy, but now, he chooses to live in his own happiness, and to these young men, his smile tells them to see the joy above any challenge they face.

* * *

2016 SPRING TRAINING

"Josiah! Why aren't you at the big league game? They didn't kick you out for hitting too many home runs did they?" one of Josiah's friends from the Spikes 2015 team teased. It was now 2016 spring training, and the Spikes player and Josiah had formed a bond while the former was rehabbing a broken hand in State College. They kept in touch over the offseason, and now they were officially reunited on the field once again.

During spring training, Josiah was given an All-Access pass to the entire MLB complex. But each day before the major league game was finished, Josiah would drop everything and ask to be carted to Practice Field Three— the minor league side of spring training.

Each day, Josiah would look up at his personal assistant—specifically assigned to cart and chauffeur Josiah around for the week—and told him he wanted to go to the practice fields. The gentleman would look at him like he had two heads. He couldn't understand why a kid would want to leave the glitz and the glamor of a Major League Baseball stadium for the chain-link fence and empty bleachers of a minor league practice field. And finally, after a puzzling few days, our assistant finally asked, "Why would you ever want to leave all this for Field Three, buddy?"

Josiah just shrugged and said in the most innocent voice a little boy could have, "It's where my friends are."

Just like that, the driver smiled, and they drove to Field Three.

"No-oo!" Josiah said to his friend while climbing on the player's lap, "I told them I'd see them tomorrow, and it was time to see you guys," he said in his distinct, muffled little voice.

"Buddy, you know all of us would kill to be on that field, right?" the player said, pointing to the stadium.

"Yeah. So?"

"So?! You just turned it down! I must say, man, that takes some guts . . . and a choice I'd never make in a million years," he said, flicking Josiah's cap down over his face. "Hey I'm going to be up soon, you think I'll hit a home run?"

"No. You're a doubles hitter."

"HA! If I hit a home run, I get your cookie after dinner. Deal?"

"Deal!"

After two sliders and a weak popup to the first baseman, the player was back on the bench faster than Josiah could blink, and they both couldn't help but let out a small giggle. Josiah climbed back on his lap and said, "It's OK, you can still have my cookie."

After the game, Josiah met the guys back at the hotel. They have a routine: Dinner at five—where Josiah eats a spoonful of rice, a half slice of turkey, and a full piece of chocolate cake by himself—cards by the pool at six, and a movie of his choice at seven.

The usual dinner crowd finished up dessert, and a group of guys headed out to the pool for their nightly game of Big Three. Cards were thrown, tempers were pushed, and friendships might be strained, but the boys finished up their rowdy "Poker Night," and Josiah jumped on a player's shoulders to catch their seven o'clock Netflix movie.

"No way, Jo, we've watched *Pirates of the Caribbean* last night and both nights before that. Johnny Depp is good, but the Black Pearl can wait," the player demanded as they entered the elevator.

Josiah laughed and twisted his ear while sitting on his shoulders.

"Ahh. Hurt me all you want! You're still gonna have to choose a different movie tonight, and that's that!"

So, as they devoured a few cookies while watching *Pirates of the Caribbean*, Dave came to the room to finish the movie and get the little man ready for bed, who was already nodding off in his recliner stuffed with every pillow in the room. The player greeted Dave at the door and said, "Pap, thank you."

"For what?" he laughed.

"For introducing us to Josiah. This game, this minor league life, it takes a part of you, man. And sometimes you just don't know if you'll ever get it back. We get so consumed by this game that sometimes we forget there's even more to life." He paused and ran his fingers through his hair, composing himself. "But this little boy—he gives us the life we've been missing, and if it weren't for you, none of us would have been introduced to Josiah, and none of us would have been able to see the light God put in Josiah. So, Pap, thank you."

* * *

I stood on the crunchy gravel of Medlar Field and thought about the players Josiah has impacted over the years. I thought about this game and how fortunate we have been to have met so many great people. But on this particular day, I looked beyond the center-field wall, and the sight of our Appalachian Mountains sent chills running up and down my arms.

It was the same backdrop I had been staring at at for every home game for two years now, but today I didn't see it the same.

I saw our family blended within her hills, and the images of my life I tried to tuck away forever started rushing through my head. All the days I spent as a child running through her woods in my only state of freedom, the lonely nights I spent at the station listening to the birds singing their final song at sunset, and all the hours I spent gazing at her through the plastic windowpane of a PICU window came rushing through me like a stampede of memories I could no longer control. I stared at her beauty. I gazed at her green and red crimson trees and marveled at her hardened paths. And I saw our little man standing tall, waving a baseball bat the very size of his own body standing in front. I took a step back, and as I looked at the mountains and the little boy who has defined our lives for so long, it now finally hit me.

Josiah was never climbing the mountain placed in our lives; Josiah *is* the mountain divinely dropped into our lives.

I looked at the mountain's eternal strength and protection given to our home, and I saw the unshakeable faith Josiah has given to our family. Like a winter, stripping the land bare until spring can break its cold, I saw the suffering and hurt our little boy went through fighting a coma no child should bear. But I also saw every step over steep and narrow trails running through the mountain's rough terrain and I couldn't help but see the same courage running through this little boy's veins.

I saw the mountains, and I saw Josiah.

I stood there with a perspective as vast as the mountains were wide, and I saw our existence not being defeated by their imprisonment but rather enhanced by the nature of their being. From here it looked like the mountains could roll forever, never truly being able to know where it begins or where it ends, and now I finally saw the same in Josiah.

For years his story has traveled, been identified by people across the nation, and as his journey grows, his impact continues way further than our human eyes can see. I believe it was all by God's design. Like the hill's ridges that remain strong after the nastiest storms, he, too, will endure, and his message will be seen long after the last tree branch is broken and the last leaf is swept away.

At that moment I finally saw it.

Josiah never climbed any mountain. He had become one.

* * *

Drenched in sweat, the once-light-gray Dri-Fit t-shirts of the players were now soggy black rags. It was a hot, muggy summer day and the July heat beating down made batting practice lethargic and a gift for these boys to be over. But as they jogged toward home plate, their tiresome looks were exchanged with excitement because there was one more round of batting practice to watch.

Josiah walked to the plate—batting gloves fastened, bat dragging behind his heels—and the players began to cheer like it was their first trip to an amusement park. I couldn't help but notice the constant joy this round of batting practice brought to not only Josiah but also the entire team all season long.

For the past few years I had watched a group of young men—fighting and striving to get out of State College and move up the ranks—for ten minutes make the game something more than just a pit stop along their bigger journey and cheer on a young boy to pursue the game he loves. It was unforgettable–for Josiah and for me.

The hot sun continued to beat down and, like always, Josiah tapped the plate twice and set his hands like Coach Sam taught him—he was ready.

With every swing and gentle ping of the bat, I savored a moment that never gets old. The chatter from the guys, the simultaneous roar with each connection, and the look on my little man's face was like I was seeing it for the first time.

The smiles from players reminded me of every person that we had the fortune of meeting: doctors, nurses, corporate workers, celebrities, minor leaguers, major leaguers, hall of famers, and everyone in between. I saw the reflection of joy Josiah had been able to bring to people during the toughest hours, and I saw the fresh breath of reality they had been searching for.

His final swing came to a close, and after he connected he took off running for first base. He hobbled in pain with every step, and the devastating reality of Progeria became visible to everyone around—but he wouldn't stop. He never does. With each grueling year, his knees continue to bulge and his ankles continue to wobble, now making running almost unbearable. His home run trot has been cut down to just a sprint to first base and still the pain on his face continues to build with each grimacing step.

But he pushes through.

He may not know it, but his painful run to first base is a message to me. It's a message to our family. For years I've only seen the pain this little boy goes through to reach first base. I look at his face and I see the agony, but I never searched beyond it. The pain our family hid from—our divided lives, our empty search for healing, and the distance we put between each other—was only the grimace on the face of a little boy running to first, but we never searched beyond the hurt. Until Josiah, we were never forced *through* the pain.

I watched our little man kick his legs and push his way to first base, but about halfway to the bag, his sneaker caught on the grass protector, and he came crashing down. Face down into the dirt, the players panicked, and I came running over and scooped him up. His elbows were scratched, blood had already started to trickle from his knee, and tears had begun to form under his eyelids. I held Josiah and the rest of the team came running over. He was hurt.

"Let's get him in the dugout and call the trainer!" I yelled, as a nasty fall for a Progeria child is like a car crash for anyone else. The team hopped into action.

"No!" Josiah yelled.

"Bubby, we need to get you checked, the trainer is—"

"Put me down!"

"Bubby, I—"

"Pap," he paused and sniffled back tears. "Put me down!"

I didn't know what to say. He was hurting and I knew it.

I held onto Jen's words of quality over quantity, but her words fell flat.

I can't do it. I can't let him go. But I know I have to.

I protect him, I take care of him, and he takes care of me. We go to baseball games and sing songs on the car radio. We watch TV and listen to Cardinals games before bedtime together. But that little boy with tears in his eyes and scrapes on his face and nose has become my world, and God has used that little boy to redirect my path in this life, to view the world with a different set of eyes, and to see people the way God sees them.

I continued to hold Josiah in my arms. I bowed my head, wishing there was a way we could just switch places, a way he could be out of his pain, and a way I could protect him. But Josiah gave me the look that only he could do. The tears were now overpowering his sniffles and flooding the corners of his eyes, but he continued to look at me with a sense of strength and said one last time, "Pap. Put. Me. Down."

I squeezed this tough little man and he squeezed me, knowing that I had to let him finish the journey he set out to bear.

So, I put him down.

I let him go.

And with a hobble in his step, Josiah touched first—a journey complete.

J-Rod put his arm around my shoulders and told me how much that run meant to him and the team. He said if the team had half of that little boy's heart, they would go undefeated. I thanked him for all he had done for Josiah. But as I stood and watched the team swarm Josiah with hugs, J-Rod and the other coaches, Darwin Morreo and Rodger LaFrancois, shook my hand, hugged me, and said, "No, thank you." At that moment, I knew. From all the lives he's touched and all the friendships he's made, Josiah's light will travel far beyond what we could ever dream. Josiah was meant to be on this earth to complete a journey far greater than the journey of just one man, but to inspire a generation to do the same in their lives—including my own.

It was now my turn.

It was now my journey to complete. My choice to make. I walked off that field and just knew; there was something I had to do.

And someone I had to see.

30

FORGIVENESS

I TURNED THE CAR off and stared at the same stone entryway I saw years ago. The sun had faded the gray stones to a sandwashed white, and they still seemed to hold up the freestanding gate to a land neither fenced nor protected. I recognized the same trees and the same stones, only aged a few decades, and I couldn't help but think they saw the same in me.

From the diagnosis to the infection, from my broken relationship with Jen to our years spent together in a hospital room, to my rejection of religion, and to my awakening of faith, this family has been cast on a journey none of us wished to explore. But as Josiah touched that base, we saw the start of a journey. We saw a little boy choose courage. We saw a little boy choose to see beyond the pain of his life to change ours.

Our lives have been blended by struggle and pain only to be conquered by love. The blessing of a special little boy named Josiah forced us into a pain we never knew existed, and we found a love we never could foster.

The love Liz has been able to share with my daughter not only brought back the devoted, passionate daughter I once knew, but it gave her hope knowing that it was OK to love again. As I searched for my faith and Josiah searched for health, our family searched for each other.

Like the strings of an unwoven basket, we broke at every crossroad. But as God continued to weave our lives together, we were forced to face every challenge as a single braid; with each twisting and hurting moment, we relied on each other and became sturdy before we could even recognize it.

I thought about family, and I thought about God's love and mercy He has shown me when I was lost and wandering in the darkness of my heart. I thought about our lives forced to see joy over misery, always choosing love over hate, and I thought about all the years I had lost choosing the latter. I thought about my love for Jen and Liz, Josiah and his big sister, Daisha, my wife, Deb, and the family that's given me a new life, and I felt the same tug on my heart from the baseball field.

I knew I had to do this.

I slammed the car door shut, turning directly to the rusted gate. My heart began to thump, and my feet started to pick up speed, matching the rhythm of the blood pumping through my veins. I walked under the trees on a mission. Once I passed the gate, my mind went blank, and I could hardly notice the leaves crunching under my boots. Another family was here, I thought, but nothing registered.

By the time I was halfway to my destination I looked down, and my hands were turning bright red. The autumn's frost had greeted us early, and I forgot my jacket in the car. But I didn't feel a thing. I finally got to the corner and saw a sign, "Fresh Flowers Only." I looked down, and there it was: a gray plaque with more algae and grass growing over it than the stone gate at the entrance—still no flowers.

I read the engraving. Guy E. Bohner. I looked at my hands, now shaking from the cold. I stood in the exact place I did almost twenty years ago at the funeral I didn't care about next to a woman I didn't care about, with the numbing frost I felt trickling up my arms exactly the way my heart had felt that day.

I looked at the forests and saw the bush slowly creeping in from the mountainside. Like the weeds once tamed and matted around his plaque now growing wildly out of control and consuming his gravesite, the bush seemed to slowly creep in and surround us as well, like we were the only two in the world together.

I drew a breath and thought about last time we were in the woods like this together. I believe we said the same amount of words as we did today. It felt the same—stagnant, questioning if we should be here, and the stories of our lives unfolded from words we couldn't say.

When I was thirteen or fourteen years old, we were hunting small game one day—one of the few things we actually did together. He said he wanted to show me something. It was way out of character for him since we usually went directly home.

I had no idea where he was taking me, and from an hour of turning on and off forest-lined dirt roads, it seemed like he didn't either. We didn't speak much, as was the norm. We just sat in silence, and I stared out the window until I felt the rev of his engine slowly coast to a stop and heard him throw the car into park. We were here—the middle of nowhere, with only old stones, cracked and withered into rubble.

He got out of the car, and I followed, but something about him was strange—something wasn't right. He didn't look at me, he didn't speak right away, but I knew this place meant more to him than it ever would to me. I looked at him, and I could see a depth of sadness I had never noticed before. He just stared at the pile of rocks, and I stared at him.

It was as if the ruins of these stones had changed him.

It was as if these stones were telling him a story he never wished to hear. It was as if these stones were the demons he was carrying around since the first time he met them. Then finally he looked at me and said this was where he grew up. This was the remains of the cabin where he spent his childhood. As he said those words, and for a brief moment in time, like a flash of light, or seeing your breath quickly disappear on a cold winter day, I sensed something different in my father.

He wasn't a man of many words, and as he turned back to the remains of the place where he once lived, he stood in silence and said nothing. He stared into the forest as if going back in time. And for a moment, it seemed as if he were remembering his childhood.

Still he said nothing. He just looked around as if reliving a childhood lost. I thought, *Is this where it all started?* His drinking himself into oblivion. His out-of-control anger. Did his father, my grandfather who died before I was born, abuse him? Did the words "I love you" ever ring through the forest where a small log cabin once stood? We stood in silence with only the wind whispering through the trees. He said nothing more.

I didn't care about his story.

Was that supposed to make up for everything he did to me? Was that supposed to make everything better? I was calloused over, and the hardened heart he carried was the one I chose to pick up. That day I knew those stones remained in his heart—and I wanted them to.

But now I stood over his grave, recalling that day and wondering if that was his message to me—if that was his way of telling me that since he failed, the cycle needed to end with me. I took another short breath and thought about my life; the pain and the hurt, my family I pushed way, the grace I received when they came back into my life, and the miracle of a little boy who gave us the message that changed our lives.

The only constant in our lives has been pain—the same pain that was hidden in a small pile of stones where a cabin once stood and was passed down to me. I saw the dark side of life and continued to follow it down a road of destruction and hurt.

I chose to let it kill us.

But then the Lord placed a little boy into our lives, a little boy who didn't have a choice in how long his life may be, but a choice in the way in which he lives it.

Josiah chooses joy.

Pain may have always been the constant in our lives, but the only constant in Josiah's life is his decision to live beyond a disease and to allow God's light to shine through him every day—and our family has followed. Josiah shows us that although we may not ever have a choice in how long our lives can be lived, we can choose how to live them. Every day we wake up, we can choose to live at the mercy of our situations or live by the mercy of the Lord.

In all pain, choose joy. In all doubt, choose faith. In all fear, choose courage. In the face of death, choose life, and above all— choose Christ.

Now, it was time for me to choose.

I looked at that man's grave and took one more breath. My hands were still shivering cold, but I couldn't feel a thing. This was something I needed to do. This was something I needed to do the first time I stood before his stone. I stared at the lettering on his plaque and said, "No more. All of it ends now."

Tears filled the corners of my eyes as I started talking, and my throat tightened.

"Just know it wasn't your fault, and it ends now. I promise you, it ends now."

Tears streamed down my face.

"I forgive you. Dad. I forgive you."

I picked my head up and drew a final steady breath in and watched my exhale burst through the crisp autumn air. I felt a weight leave with the breath that exited my lungs. I saw the mountainside, I saw my family, and I finally smiled, thinking about Josiah and his name.

The name that could only mean, "God has healed."

AUTHOR'S NOTE

I N THE SUMMER OF 2015, Josiah and I were in the dugout at a State College Spikes game. A young ballplayer for the minor league affiliate of the St. Louis Cardinals, the Peoria Chiefs, stepped into the dugout. Being injured in a game some weeks before, he was in State College for rehab. He introduced himself: "Hi, I'm Jake Gronsky." We continued to talk for a few more minutes, bantered about baseball, our faith in Christ, and then I discovered his home was in Danville, PA—the same town in which Josiah had spent his first two years of life confined to a hospital bed. Jake lived less than a mile from the window I stared out of wondering if that was the last view Josiah and I would ever share together. From that point forward, I needed to find out more, and our friendship began to grow.

Fast-forward to March of the 2016 St. Louis Cardinals Spring Training Camp in Jupiter, FL. We were hanging out with all the players, including our new friend Jake. We'd spent the previous off-season together, getting coffee, sharing the Gospel, and Jake had even come to Josiah's doctor's appointments—never missed one. But what happened next is a ballplayer's worst nightmare. I got a call from Jake: "Dave, I've been cut from the Cardinals. I'm going home tomorrow morning." It was tough for all of us, especially Jo, but little did we know the decision to let Jake go would be the beginning of an adventure we never could have imagined.

Late spring 2016, I was with Jake and his dad for a game at Bloomsburg University's baseball field. We had talked a lot about Josiah and what had transpired in his life to that point. Every Thursday night we would get coffee and I told him our story—I told *him* the story. The game continued on, and I mentioned I was trying to write a book about Josiah but was struggling to find the words to articulate everything I couldn't say for the past thirty years.

With the speed of a ballplayer moving on the field to make a play, Jake turned in his seat and looked me in the eyes. With the same excitement of a player who just hit a grand slam or hit the winning run in the bottom of the ninth, he said to me, "I want to help."

Thus, the writing began.

We started wanting to write a story about Josiah and his love of baseball. Little did we know the story would evolve into something more than just a biography. It was becoming a story of early childhood struggles. Of faith and family and forgiveness. And most importantly, a story of a boy named Josiah, whom God placed within our family.

I believe all the events that had happened to this point did not happen by accident. From meeting Jake in a dugout after a season-ending injury, to his release from the Cardinals organization, to the writing of this book, God has had His hand in all of it.

But then again, this is a story of a struggling family and a boy who was so ill that no doctor thought he could ever survive, culminating in a boy's love for the game of baseball. God has *always* had His hand in all of it.

Dave Bohner

THE JOSIAH WE KNOW

W HEN FIRST MEETING JOSIAH, the moment seemed unreal. I remember that day like it was yesterday. I sat down to see this small six-year-old boy dancing around in front of me, laughing with his high-pitched voice. He was full of character, glowing with happiness, and ready to play baseball in the yard for hours. I did not expect this day to turn into six years of a family growing to love one another, rising to the challenges of everyday life.

Most people only meet Josiah once, maybe a few times. Not many people get to know the true Josiah, the Josiah we see daily, through the good days, bad days, and the days in between. The love that we have all felt over the last six years has been something that none of us will forget.

When the kids were younger they were constantly full of energy, always playing games, wrestling with one another—Daisha on the floor with Josiah hopping on top of her—while we held our breath warning Daisha to be careful with Josiah. Already at the ages of six and seven, the two of them had a huge size difference, with Daisha quickly growing—she is now taller than we are! Of course they have always been typical siblings; there was not one day of their younger years that we did not hear Josiah bellow out, "Daisha!" followed by Daisha yelling back, "Brother!!!" You know, the typical fighting over what was on the television or who had the player one Wii remote first. Weekend trips to go shopping, to carnivals, or to visit family were always filled with music and both kids singing at the top of their lungs to whatever new song was the rage at the time. No matter how different Daisha and Josiah have been, they were always dedicated to one another.

Deep down, Josiah is just a normal kid, even though at times, when in public, people tend to stare, point, or say things that most people would not say out loud that leave him frustrated. It only took one night waiting in line for ice cream when a woman approached us and said, "That's a real interesting kid you got there! What does he have, a disease or something?" to bring me into a rage. However, Josiah's strength and ability to just look at me and say, "Calm down, Liz, it's OK," left me in awe. He has always been calm in these moments, and although at times we can see the frustration, he rolls with the punches and moves on, even if we struggle with that ourselves.

Josiah has always been the glue that brings us together; he always is a shoulder to cry on and shows how much he cares when times are tough. When the time came for one of our family dogs to cross over he was there by our side, giving Fiona one last pat on her head saying, "I'll see you soon, Fiona," and making sure he was available for endless hugs in the days after that dreaded vet visit. Despite Josiah's physical limitations he pushes the people he loves when they, too, are experiencing physical limitations. Whether it was his Nana, who experienced many limitations and is wheelchair bound, or Daisha when she sprained her ankle. When I experienced a bad break to my leg he was there with me. He held my hand after my surgery, stood by patiently watching an assisting Jen change my bandages for the first time, and pushing me to get my butt off of the recliner for physical therapy.

Other than baseball, Josiah loves cooking. The young man spends his days watching Food Network and has seen every single episode of *Pioneer Woman* and *Guy's Grocery Games*. Every day I hear, "Liz, Can you make that?" So, one Christmas time, thanks to Grandma Melanie and Uncle Jimmy and Aunt Shelly, he got his own set of small "Josiah size" cooking tools, from spatulas, spoons, knives and tongs, to cutting boards and bowls. He was thrilled. He was at the table and stove with me daily, cooking, baking, and flipping pancakes in his own chef's apron.

Josiah has always been a mama's boy and followed her everywhere; that is, up until last year when he realized that he has grown up. He was always hugging her, saying "I love you, Mama" a couple times a day. Always insisting on sitting behind her when we drove, so she was always in eyesight. The bond between them is like none I've ever seen before. I've never seen a mom so keen to know exactly what her son needs to feel better at any moment. No matter where we eat he shares her plate. He is truly a mama's boy.

Like all teenage boys, Josiah enjoys video games, from Madden and MLB: The Show, to Injustice and Battlefront; he is always bugging to play. There may have been some weekend nights that even I lost track of time and was shocked when it was suddenly 12:30 a.m. and we were still playing. Josiah loves when his friends come over. Bringing his buddies over gives Josiah the power to do the things we typically say "no" to. With a big guy by his side, he has had couches flipped over to make elaborate forts, had Nerf gun battles, and has been able to polish off an entire bag of chips and candy before anyone noticed. When these days happen Josiah hates when the time comes to say goodbye to his buddies; you can see the sadness in his eyes when this epic time is over. We always promise a next time, so he knows that these good times can happen again. Josiah is a master negotiator: When you tell him "five minutes," he wants eight—and often gets his way—although sometimes we do have to say "no," as you do to all kids.

When it all boils down, Josiah is really just a typical kid wrapped up in this miracle that no one expected to happen. He is strong, brave, and always there for everyone. We could not have been luckier in this life than to have experienced his love and his light. We continue to encourage Josiah to live his life to the fullest, and will always help his mom with what she set out to do from the beginning: "While we can, let's just let Josiah be a kid."

Liz Pysher with Jen Viera

ACKNOWLEDGMENTS

WE WOULD LIKE TO thank all the people who helped shape and form this book: Dr. Colleen Walsh, Bonnie Tharp, Children's Miracle Network, nurse Stephanie Wesner, Kim Gummel, and all the nurses and medical staff at Geisinger's Janet Weis Children's hospital, Dr. Scorpio, Collin Radack, Nick Thompson, Diane Thompson and the Thompson family, Danny Diekroger, Chase Raffield, Michael Pritchard, the St. Louis Cardinals organization and media, the State College Spikes, Oliver Marmol, CJ Beatty, Mitch Harris, Johnny "J-Rod" Rodriguez, Joe Putnum, Steve Jones, Jason "JD" Dambach, Roger LaFrancois, Scott Walker, and everyone else at the State College Spikes.

We want to specifically thank Ben Houser and the entire ESPN *E:60* crew. Without his guidance and his belief in our family, this story may not be here today.

A very special thanks to our close friend Andy Long, at W & L Subaru, who helps take us not only to Cardinals spring training camp every year but anywhere Josiah wants to travel. We are forever grateful for his generosity.

There are so many people we may have missed, but we cannot thank you enough for being in our lives. The relationships we have created over the years mean the world to us, and we thank you for your friendship.

And finally, over the past eighteen months, we have diligently attempted to write this story as historically accurate as possible.

From Dave: I myself could not have done this alone without the help of Jake and my immediate family, Deb, Jen, Liz, Daisha, and, of course, Josiah.

From Jake: I'd like to thank my mom, dad, and brother for challenging me in every step of this journey.

Once our story was written, we cannot thank our editor, Kate Matson, enough for the hours she spent meticulously shaping and polishing our manuscript into a book. Thank you for believing in this story, and thank you for pushing us every step of the way.

And also a heartfelt thanks to all our friends who encouraged us to push onward. They told us the same thing Josiah always tells us:

"Never give up!"

RESOURCES

Doctor Coleen Walsh, medical consult

Pastor Mark Gittens of High Hope Church: spiritual consult

"An Inspiring few minutes," *Centre Daily Times*, 2013

If I Could Just Sit With You Awhile by Dennis Jernigan.
http://www.dennisjernigan.com/

Channel 6 WJAC Ashley Chase
https://www.youtube.com/watch?time_continue=2&v=-ZQ1Yb7QdDo

Job 13:15 – King James Version

James 4:14 – King James Version

Romans 5:3-5 – New Living Translation

ABOUT THE AUTHORS

DAVE BOHNER is a husband, father, grandfather, and retired welder who has served in the PA Air National Guard, United States Air Force. He is currently president of the Hegins Area Ambulance Association and has been a medical technician for the past twenty-seven years. He loves the game of baseball, meeting new people, and above all, Jesus.

JOSIAH VIERA is thirteen years old and just finished first year of junior high school. He loves God, baseball, dancing, and hanging out with friends. Josiah is an honorary bench coach for the

Authors (from left to right) Jake Gronsky, Josiah Viera, and Dave Bohner.

State College Spikes, the newly 'hired' bench coach for the Tri-Valley Junior High baseball team, and an honorary member of the St. Louis Cardinals. Every day, Josiah's goal is to enjoy life and to simply have fun!

JAKE GRONSKY is a former professional baseball player in the St. Louis Cardinals organization. Jake now works with former and current professional athletes, writing stories of faith, courage, and perseverance. He lives in Philadelphia, Pennsylvania, and can be found on Twitter @Jake_Gronsky or contacted by email at Gronsky.Jake@gmail.com.

Made in the USA
Middletown, DE
10 July 2018